THE LAST VICTORIANS
by
Arthur A. Baumann
(A. A. B.)

"Our clock strikes when there is a change from hour to hour; but no hammer in the Horologe of Time peals through the Universe when there is a change from Era to Era."—
CARLYLE.

Philadelphia
J. B. Lippincott Company
1927

MADE AND PRINTED IN GREAT BRITAIN
BY THE STANHOPE PRESS LTD., ROCHESTER, KENT

CONTENTS

		PAGE
1.	INTRODUCTION: THE VICTORIAN TRADITION	13
2.	QUEEN VICTORIA'S MIDDLE YEARS	29
3.	DISRAELI'S MERIDIAN	41
4.	THE MARQUIS OF SALISBURY	59
5.	SIR WILLIAM HARCOURT	87
6.	VISCOUNT GOSCHEN	101
7.	THE BALFOUR–CHAMBERLAIN PARTNERSHIP	121
8.	LORD RANDOLPH CHURCHILL	145
9.	WALTER BAGEHOT	165
10.	ANTHONY TROLLOPE	185
11.	BENJAMIN JOWETT	197
12.	MR. "JIM" LOWTHER	209
13.	GEORGE WYNDHAM	217
14.	LORD CHIEF JUSTICE COLERIDGE	225
15.	SIR HENRY FOWLER	233
16.	SIR JOHN GORST	241
17.	SIR MICHAEL HICK-BEACH	249
18.	HENRY LABOUCHERE	257
19.	CHARLES STEWART PARNELL	267
20.	VISCOUNT GREY	275
21.	THE EARL OF OXFORD	283
22.	THE STATESMAN'S END	307

LIST OF ILLUSTRATIONS

THE MARQUIS OF SALISBURY		*..Frontispiece*
THE EARL OF BEACONSFIELD	*Facing page*	61
LETTER FROM THE MARQUIS OF SALISBURY	,, ,,	80
JOSEPH CHAMBERLAIN	,, ,,	123
LORD RANDOLPH CHURCHILL	,, ,,	147
ANTHONY TROLLOPE	,, ,,	187
GEORGE WYNDHAM	,, ,,	221
VISCOUNT GREY	,, ,,	279
THE EARL OF OXFORD	,, ,,	285

PREFACE

Of everyone of the personalities here portrayed or criticised, except Trollope and Bagehot, I can say

"sic ille manus, sic ora gerebat,"

that is, I have seen and heard them all, and spoken with most of them.

A. A. B.

1927
44 Hyde Park Square.

The Victorian Tradition

"Some ages are marked as sentimental, others stand conspicuous as rational. The Victorian age was happier than most in the flow of both these currents into a common stream of vigorous and effective talent. . . The rational prevented the sentimental from falling into pure emotional."—LORD MORLEY'S *Recollections*.

THE VICTORIAN TRADITION

CENTURIES are, we know, artificial divisions of time, and I have not discovered by whom or for what purpose that method of chronology was first adopted. It does, however, seem that at the end of a period, roughly approximating to a hundred years, a new generation, with new habits and modes of speech, insensibly emerges into existence. Modern historians, like Green and Trevelyan, are apt to sneer at the idea that the births and deaths of kings and queens have anything to do with the destiny of mankind. Those who, like myself, believe in personal rather than tendencious records, and agree with Disraeli that biography is the best history, will find their theory confirmed by the fact that for the last four centuries, at least, changes of tradition have been synchronous with the deaths of British Sovereigns. It must be so generally, because when a powerful monarch dies, there pass with him or her a group of courtiers, who set the fashion, and a group of ministers, who govern the State. The death of Elizabeth ended the Tudor tradition. The Stuart tradition lasted, with the interruption of the Cromwellian decade, until the death of Anne in 1714. The Hanoverian tradition lasted until after Waterloo, and the death of George III in 1820. The painful interregnum filled by the sons of George III was closed by the accession of Victoria in 1837. At the end of the last century, between 1898 and 1903, there died Mr. Gladstone, Queen Victoria, and Lord Salisbury, and with them was interred the Victorian tradition. Not of course sharply or immediately, for some of the great Queen's servants, Morley, Harcourt, and Bannerman, survived her, and two, Lords Oxford and Grey, are still with us. King Edward, with his unerring instinct, felt that some relaxation of Court etiquette was necessary, but he did his best, though unsuccessfully, to maintain the Victorian tradition in politics. That, however, was not possible after Lord Salisbury's death. The distraction, or more plainly the destruction, of the Unionist party in the hands of Messrs. Arthur Balfour and Joseph Chamberlain led to the polls of 1905, and after that the Victorian tradition perished utterly.

I am a Victorian Tory, naked and unashamed. I make no pretence to impartiality, or attempt to defend my prejudices. I do but touch the Great War in connection with Lords Oxford and Grey. Enough has been written on that subject by greater pens than mine. Armageddon apart, everything done after 1906 is for me a step on the easy slope that leads unlimited democracy to its nadir of helplessness and corruption.

The Trades Disputes Act contradicts the principles of personal freedom and equality before the law, and places our industrial system at the mercy of the trade unions. The Finance Act of 1910 and the unfair incidence of war taxation, have led to the break up of landed estates, and the ruin of the territorial aristocracy. The Parliament Act has placed us under single-chamber government. The Reform Act of 1918, that crowning exhibition of sentiment and recklessness, rushed through Parliament without debate in the last year of the war, added twelve million voters to the register, including the recipients of parish relief and the wives of existing voters. The surrender of five-sixths of Ireland to the party of murder and treason by Unionist statesmen completes the tale.

What do I mean by the Victorian tradition? During Victoria's reign the government of the country was conducted by men round whom the confidence of the country had gathered during many years of public service. Their characters and accomplishments were known to everyone, and they took their trust seriously and reverently. Burke said of Admiral Keppel, " there was something high about him." There was something high about statesmen like Goschen, Harcourt, Beach, Salisbury, Hartington, Balfour, Morley, who governed England during the last twenty years of the last century. To the early Victorian period, between 1840 and 1880, belong Macaulay, Peel, Cobden, Bright, Palmerston, Gladstone, Disraeli, Lowe, Derby, surely a constellation of orators such as no country ever produced before. Nor was it only of eloquent leaders that this age was prolific; it was distinguished by the number of independent members of Parliament such as Molesworth, Burdett, Grote, Roebuck, Stuart Mill, Horsman, men of letters, and free-spoken country gentlemen, who would have scorned to be told what they were to say, and how they were to vote.

I may be wrong in placing the Augustan age of parliamentary government in Victoria's reign. I like to remember Cromwell's adjuration to his petitioners to bethink them, in Christ's name, that they might be wrong. I will therefore call the corroborative testimony of, not another Tory, but of a Whig, " of purest ray serene." Sir Almeric Fitzroy, descendant of a Whig duke, was for thirty years Clerk of the Privy Council, and for that time lived very near the rose.

It is, of course, essential that the Clerk of the Privy Council should be a gentleman, because his relations with the Sovereign and the Lord President of the Council are intimate and confidential. He is a liaison officer between the ceremonial and executive parts of the Constitution; and though the size of the Council called Privy, which has some 250 members, has necessarily deprived it of power, there are always some dozen of its number who know everything that is to be known about Kings and Cabinets.

Sir Almeric betrays no confidences and makes no unkind personal observations. But the two closely packed volumes of his memoirs* are in themselves a very serious indiscretion, none the less grave because it is doubtful whether the author has written for our amendment or our amusement.

On almost every page Sir Almeric Fitzroy reveals the fact that after the death of Lord Salisbury, the

*Memoirs, Sir Almeric Fitzroy. Hutchinson. 2 vols.

government of England was conducted with a levity, a personal rancour, and an unscrupulousness, that sometimes outrages decency, and often staggers credibility. Such a revelation of carelessness and extravagance is dangerous knowledge.

Sir Almeric, with a personal admiration of Mr. Balfour and an earnest desire to be fair to Mr. Chamberlain, strains his courtly vocabulary to its limit to conceal his contempt for the weakness and sophistry of the Tory leader and his anger at the ruthless indiscipline of his Radical colleague. Mr. Balfour began as a Free Fooder, then announced that he had no settled convictions either way, and finally was driven into declaring that Tariff Reform was the first plank in the constructive platform of the Conservative Party.

Mr. Balfour paid a visit to Esher Place, and upon being asked by his hostess, Lady Helen Vincent (as she was then), whether he would take tea or coffee, replied that he didn't care which. " Oh! I see, you have no settled convictions on the point." The random shaft, drawn by a lovely hand, pierced the mail of the philosopher, and Sir Almeric tells us that Mr. Balfour was visibly " nettled."

Great parties are not kept together by " the gossamer web " of Socratic subtlety, nor are they to be bludgeoned into following the flag of a political corsair. The odd thing is that when the outside world could see that the Tory Party was heading straight for destruction, Taper Hood, better known as the Pink 'Un, and Tadpole Hughes, the helpless agent at the Central

Office, assured their chiefs and the Carlton Club that the Radicals couldn't even form a Government!

Such boastful incompetence met the punishment it deserved. Sir Henry Campbell-Bannerman formed, in December, 1905, the strongest Government, as regards individual capacity, of modern times, and, by the folly of the Unionist leaders and the accident of war, one of the longest lived. The new Prime Minister had been trained under Mr. Gladstone and Sir William Harcourt, and for two years the gravity and decorum of public life were kept up.

With the Premiership of Mr. Asquith the reign of laxity began. Then was the era of Christian names all round. From the hour when a famous financier addressed Mr. Balfour as " Arthur " in a club, and Tory and Radical leaders played bridge together, " the game of lor and order was up." The phrase which Bismarck applied to Salisbury, " a lath painted to look like iron," was far more applicable to Mr. Asquith. He could not, or would not, control the slap-dash methods of Messrs. Churchill and Lloyd George.

Side by side with the financial mess of the 1909 Budget proceeded the bargaining with Mr. John Redmond over Home Rule and the House of Lords. The 80 Irish Nationalists knew that as long as the House of Lords retained its constitutional powers no Home Rule Bill could pass. They also knew that their 80 votes could turn out the Government. Even when they had, by means which we shall never know until Lord Oxford and the King are dead, tied the hands of the House of Lords, the Government found that they had forgotten Ulster, and began shilly-shallying, not knowing, like Macbeth, whether to go back or forward. General Seely, a Tory deserter, thought of the Army, but found the officers wouldn't march. Mr. Churchill, another Tory deserter, sent a wireless order to the Navy, which he almost immediately revoked. Never a word did anybody hear about the consequences to poor England and Scotland. On this wretched scene of personal squabbling and parochial politics descended Armageddon. Even then personal rivalry and indecision continued. Lord Morley, discussing Cabinets with the Clerk of the Privy Council in 1912, said, " One hears this or that criticised on public grounds, when one knows that it is merely the expression of A's dislike of B."

The only member of the Government who worked seriously at his job, and to whose brains and courage the country owed the landing of the Expeditionary Force, was Lord Haldane. Yet he was discarded on the formation of the first Coalition in May, 1915, owing to the jealousy of some of his colleagues, and the fear of the rabble who mobbed him and broke his windows. Revenge is a dish which is best eaten cold, and eight years later Lord Haldane was again on the Woolsack when Mr. Asquith was rejected by Paisley.

On the expulsion of the Lord Chancellor the Prime Minister surpassed himself in casualness. Being away from town, he sent a wireless message to the King submitting Lord Buckmaster's name for the Great Seal!

Fancy Lord Beaconsfield or Mr. Gladstone sending a wireless message to Queen Victoria that somebody should be appointed Lord Chancellor!

From 1916 to 1922 Mr. Lloyd George was dictator. Though in the summer of 1918, the Prime Minister knew that the duration of the war was an affair of months, and though he was repeatedly warned by the Home Office, the Board of Trade and the Ministry of Labour that the demobilisation of five million men would require the most elaborate preparations and precautions, nothing whatever was done to meet the emergency. It was only when threatening crowds began to march from the East End on the Ministry of Labour in Whitehall that the public money began to fly. Then it was discovered that nobody knew what to do except to bribe somebody to go away or to stay where he was.

On January 8, 1919, there is this entry in the Clerk of the Council's diary: " I learnt from Stamfordham through the telephone that all hope of a Council this week must be abandoned. He found a most chaotic condition prevailing at No. 10. I asked him whether, with his knowledge of Downing Street, he was surprised, at which he laughed."

How can such a system produce great statesmen? I do not ignore the fact that since the break up of the Coalition in 1922, there has been a great improvement in manners under Mr. Baldwin, at any rate in ministerial circles. The Government of England is no longer treated as a gamble or an exciting farce. But what the

Government has gained in seriousness it seems to have lost in strength. Its striking power has gone; subordination has disappeared; the Government is unable to prevent an avowed Bolshevik from holding up the industry of the country for nine months. It is unable to say No to any demand on the public purse. These things suggest the interesting question, whether as we approach universal democracy, great statesmen will any longer be producible commodities.

Goldwin Smith, in his once famous essay on Cromwell, observed that the importance of great men in history becomes less as civilization goes on. " A Timon or an Attila towers unapproachably above his horde; but in the last great struggle which the world has seen the Cromwell was not a hero, but an intelligent and united nation." This is an allusion to Abraham Lincoln, for these essays were written in 1867. " And to whatever age they may belong, the greatest, the most god-like of men are men, not gods. They are the offspring, though the highest offspring, of their age."

If Cromwell escaped the intoxication of power, and bore himself as the trustee of God; if amidst the temptations of arbitrary rule, he preserved his reverence for law; it was because he was one of a religious and law-loving people. That great men are the creatures, not the creators of their age, put shortly, is the thesis of Goldwin Smith. If it was true in the seventeenth century, how much truer is it in the twentieth?

Pitt, the son of Chatham, is the last of Goldwin

Smith's *Three English Statesmen*. William Pitt became Chancellor of the Exchequer and Leader of the House of Commons in 1783, at the age of twenty-three and he was Prime Minister at the age of twenty-four. Surely, people used to say, here was a heaven-born, or a heaven-sent statesman; here was a miracle of genius! William Pitt was an extraordinarily clever youth; but if you consider that he was the son of the Earl of Chatham, who had died a few years before, in a sunset of glory, and if you recall the conditions of the political world at that time, there was nothing miraculous about it.

In order to realise the politics of that hour, you need only imagine the Carlton and Reform Clubs, next to one another in Pall Mall, containing the entire political world, as disputing, dividing, and settling the Government of England between the Committees of the two establishments, with a large secret service fund supplied partly by the dukes, partly by the Treasury, and partly by Buckingham Palace. With that system, a boy Premier is no such wonder. But how completely Pitt was the creature of his age is proved by his abandonment of all the principles with which he entered public life and of the most important measures of his first Administration. Pitt began, as became his father's son, as a Whig and a student of Adam Smith. From the fact that Chatham's picture hangs in the hall of the Carlton Club it is possible that its members think he was a Tory. The elder Pitt was an advanced Whig, and would have been horrified to hear of his son turning Tory. During his first four years the youthful Minister introduced a Reform Bill for abolishing by purchase the rotten boroughs and for free trade with Ireland, and prepared himself for a stretch of peace and economy. By the close of the sixth year he was forced to become a Tory Imperialist. His surrender, however, was no sordid or squalid affair. He was not conquered by a caucus, by a cheap press, or the " yea and nay of general ignorance." He bowed to Burke and the French Revolution.

It is necessary to distinguish between heroes and great men. To constitute heroism there must be action; no mere writer or speaker ever was a hero, for, as Byron asked, who that could act would write? Missolonghi, not " Don Juan," made Byron a hero. The hero must also sacrifice himself, I think, unto death, for a cause from which he draws no material advantage.

Nelson, we are all agreed, was a hero; but how would it have been with him if he had lived to be made a duke, ageing on a large pension at Merton with Emma? Worse still, if he had become a politician? Marlborough survived Blenheim to be tried for peculation. Wellington outlived Waterloo by thirty-five years, to sink into a commonplace partisan.

Looking back at the great war, I see only two heroes, and they were women. Edith Cavell knew well that in helping her countrymen to escape from the Germans she was, according to the laws of war, liable to be shot at dawn, and she was shot. Elsie Inglis, being a doctor, realized clearly that in fighting the typhus epidemic in Serbia she could not hope to save her own life. Her only reward was the knowledge that came to her before death that she had helped to save many Serbians. Well does Mr. David Masters say in *The Conquest of Disease*, a wonderful book, that "Dr. Elsie Inglis was a very gallant woman, and her fight with typhus is one of the most glorious pages in medical history."

Mass production, with its resultant standardisation, is obviously against the production of great men. " In the bare and level plain of democracy every ant-heap is a mountain and every thistle is a forest tree." That was Robert Lowe's picturesque way of putting, in one of his speeches against the extension of the franchise in 1867, the fact that what is called equality, as produced by legislation, is a dreary, monotonous uniformity. A great man is, as has been said, the creature of his age, but a creature of exaggerated egotism, a magnifying mirror. The tendency of an age of multiplied competition and perverted values is to smother emergence, and to distract the applause or recognition of struggling greatness.

There are ten thousand novels published every year, I am told. How many Austens and Thackerays and Trollopes pass undetected in that crowd ? Some of " the best sellers " I find it impossible to read, while often I come across a novel by an unknown, or third-rate (in the publisher's estimation) writer, which is to my taste as good as the best of the last century.

Take politics, the noblest arena for the testing of

brains and character. Is it not true that while there are some brilliant, eloquent, wise patriots in both Houses of Parliament, the best are not quite great men? Everybody respects, and many admire Mr. Baldwin. He is the kind of Minister who in the eighteenth century would have been referred to in the Royal closet as " notre bon Baldwin." He may be classed with Addington and Liverpool: but surely not with Canning and Disraeli? Lord Birkenhead and Mr. Churchill excite the daily wonder of the spectators by their feats on the political trapeze: they " wear without co-rival " all the honours of the Parliamentary field. But how many competent judges would dispute the assertion that they are not quite great men? Is not Lord Oxford the king of the Not-quites, with Mr. Lloyd George attendant as the great Might-have been?

Take the greatest war of all time, when whole nations took the field in the place of small professional armies. There were five armies under the British command, each one as big as the army commanded at Waterloo by Wellington. Yet who can name a really great soldier, I mean of the Marlborough-Wellington-Bonaparte class, thrown up by this Armageddon? The Battle of Jutland is the subject of angry dispute to this hour. But no one contends that it was a Trafalgar. Is there a Kemble, a Kean, a Siddons, or an Irving on the stage? No; but the general level of acting is raised. Quite so: we live among the Not-Quites and the Just-Nots.

I know there have been brave men after as well as

before Agamemnon; that you must stand far off if you want to see the height and shape of the mountain, and all that. But how are great men to be created by an age which pours millions into the pockets of face-contortionists, and prize-fighters: which thinks a Rugby back a greater man than a Cabinet Minister or a Judge: which crams the streets from Charing Cross to the Ritz to catch a glimpse of Chaplin or Fairbanks; and which turns its back with cold contempt upon the rest, the artistic and intellectual remnant? So ends my catechism. What the new generation may have in store for the world I do not know. Progress, the men of philosophy and science tell us, is the advance from status to contract. For the last twenty years we have been retreating from contract to status. Is it too much to hope that, if we must retrogress, we may at least recover some of the civic virtue of the last century?

Queen Victoria's Middle Years

QUEEN VICTORIA'S MIDDLE YEARS

THE interest of Mr. Buckle's edition of Queen Victoria's letters* is somewhat marred by the obvious fact that they are the remainder-biscuit out of a chest that has been ransacked by rapacious experts. Mr. Buckle himself in his six volumes of the Life of Disraeli is admittedly the chief of these raiders; Lord Morley, in his three volumes on Gladstone, is a good second; while following in their wake we have the Life of Lord Granville by Lord FitzMaurice, the Life of Lord Clarendon by Sir Herbert Maxwell, the Lives of Archbishop Tait and Lord Cranbrook, and last, but by no means least, Sir Sidney Lee's King Edward VII.

These are heavy drafts upon the Windsor Archives; so that presumably Mr. Buckle's volumes* are meant to evolve for the instruction of the public a still more intimate view of Queen Victoria's character. If that be the intention I cannot help saying that many of the letters written in the first years of the Queen's widowhood had better not have been published. Why dwell upon the weakest and most unhappy period of anybody's life in detail? The Great Queen is seen at her worst in the six years that followed the death of the Prince Consort. I feel about some of her letters of this volume very much what I felt about the publication of the senile love-letters of Lord Beaconsfield. In both cases one or two letters would surely have been enough.

**Letters of Queen Victoria*, 1862-1878. John Murray.

That the Queen of England, at the age of forty-two, in the very prime of life, surrounded by a large and affectionate family, guided in political business by the most courteous and sagacious statesmen in the world, ruling over a loyal and prosperous Empire, should describe herself as a crushed, lone, helpless widow, whose one wish was to follow her husband to a better world, is undignified, and unworthy of her station. The exaggerated language in which Victoria paints her morbid passion of bereavement is not only addressed to her relatives and her children, but to her Ministers, to Palmerston, Russell, and Gladstone. In her later years the Queen showed great power of self-restraint, of endurance, and determination. There was only one living person, perhaps, who could have taught the Queen the duty of controlling these feelings—namely, her uncle, King Leopold, who unfortunately encouraged her in what was really a form of self-indulgence. These early letters are written in a stilted and hysterical style; and after pages of them, it was with unspeakable delight that I came across a letter from " Vicky " (the Crown Princess of Prussia) who writes : " Things here are in such a mess as never was." There was another prejudice which contributed greatly to the Queen's unpopularity in these years. A Sovereign who is afraid of crowds is like a sailor who is sea-sick, or a nurse who faints at the sight of blood. Victoria was afraid of crowds in her early widowhood, and consequently hated London, and would never, if she could possibly help it, sleep so much as a night at Buckingham Palace, always returning after her Drawing-rooms in the afternoon to Windsor. Londoners bitterly resented this avoidance of their city, of which they are justly proud. Even Windsor Castle, the glory of England, the Queen wrote of as " a living grave."

Nor can it be said that the historical interest of the events with which the Queen was called upon to cope is absorbing, for the simple reason that the ground has been traversed over and over again in the very biographies to which I have above alluded. Indeed, whoever writes about the Duchies of Schleswig-Holstein, should be heavily fined. We all know that Russell and Palmerston made fools of themselves about the Duchies, having first strutted before Europe as the protectors of Denmark, and having finally sneaked out of the consequences of their words. Devoted as she was to Alexandra, Princess of Wales, the Queen was decidedly pro-Prussian at the outset of the quarrel, though after the annexation, and still more after the war upon Austria in 1866, she began to write to Vicky about the " infamy of Prussia." The best letters in the volume are those of the Crown Princess, afterwards the Empress Frederick, who gives a vivid, but just, account of her difficult position under the eye of Bismarck. Queen Victoria's views on the foreign politics of Europe, written to her daughter, to the Kings of Prussia and Belgium, and to her Ministers, are sound and well-expressed; but it is lamentable to observe how little effect they had on the course of events.

It will interest the present generation to know Queen Victoria's real opinion of Lord Palmerston. Just after his death she wrote to her uncle, the King of the Belgians : " He had many valuable qualities, though many bad ones, and we had, God knows, terrible trouble with him over foreign affairs. Still, as Prime Minister, he managed affairs at home well, and behaved to me well ; but I never liked him, or could ever the least respect him, nor could I forget his conduct on a certain occasion to my Angel. He was very vindictive, and personal feeling influenced his political acts very much." It was only when, in 1866, the Conservatives turned out Gladstone on the Reform Bill, that the Queen began to be aware of Disraeli. In an extract from her Journal, which, by the way, is more interesting than her letters, the Queen notes : " Saw Mr. Disraeli after tea, who spoke of the great Reform meeting on the 3rd, also of reform in general. . . He was amiable, and clever, but is a strange man." Strange indeed must that exotic figure have seemed in the prim circle of a Victorian Court ! But it is extraordinary how Victoria expanded and mellowed under the warmth of Disraeli's sympathy and tact. Here was a second, though a very different, and more stimulating, Lord Melbourne ! In a long letter to Her Majesty in 1868, arguing against the promotion of Tait from London to Canterbury, there is one of Disraeli's most characteristic touches : " There is in his idiosyncrasy a strange fund of enthusiasm, a quality which ought never to be possessed by an

Archbishop of Canterbury or a Prime Minister of England. The Bishop of London sympathizes with everything that is earnest; but what is earnest is not always true; on the contrary, error is often more earnest than truth." What could Victoria have thought of this cynicism? In no department of her duties did the Queen's common sense and knowledge of men come out more strongly than in the ecclesiastical appointments, where she nearly always opposed Disraeli, who had the sagacity to yield.

Queen Victoria has often been praised for brains and influence which she did not possess. It is said, for instance, that her letters show her to have been a great foreign stateswoman. The surprising thing is that, considering her position as a Sovereign of what was at that time the greatest empire in the world, and considering her relationships, she had in fact so little influence upon the great political events that occurred during her reign. Her grandfather was the King of Hanover, as was her uncle, and her daughter was married to the Crown Prince of Prussia, afterwards Emperor of Germany. Her husband was a member of the House of Coburg. If anywhere, Queen Victoria ought to have had a favourable hearing in Germany, and some influence over the policy of that country. As a matter of fact she had none. Victoria was an honest woman, and she said openly that Germany was the country of her family, for which she had a natural predilection. At the opening of the Schleswig-Holstein dispute she was pro-German, although not to the length of going to war; but when she saw the design of Bismarck to annex those countries, she began to protest. She wrote familiar letters to the King of Prussia, who was a noodle, and who handed her letters to Bismarck, and we can imagine the sneer with which the man of blood and iron read the Englishwoman's plaintive efforts on the side of peace. Ten years later, at the outbreak of the Franco-German war, Queen Victoria, with all her information from inside sources, like the letters of her daughter the Crown Princess, was as much in the dark as the man in the street as to the real origin of the conflict. On the surface it appeared that the French were the aggressors, and therefore the majority of the people with their Sovereign were pro-German. It was not till long afterwards that the world discovered that Bismarck had secretly instigated the Hollenzollern candidature for the throne of Spain, and had mutilated, or forged, the Ems telegram which led to the declaration of war by France. After Sedan and during the siege of Paris, Victoria wrote nice kindly letters to the new Emperor, and his wife Augusta, and to her daughter, urging clemency and generosity upon the conquerors, without the slightest effect upon the conduct of Moltke and Bismarck. It may be admitted that Queen Victoria helped by writing to the Tsar of Russia and to her own Ministers to prevent the monstrous crime of a second war on France in 1875, which there is no doubt that Bismarck contemplated. But the British and Russian governments had decided to stop it, and the man who contributed to the result more than anyone else was Sir Robert Morier, who on his way to St. Petersburg as Ambassador had a royal procession through France as " l'homme qui roulait Bismarck."

In the Turko-Russian war of 1877 Queen Victoria took a very violent part against Russia. There can be no doubt that if the Queen had had her way, and had wielded the power which her panegyrists ascribe to her, she would have plunged England into war on the side of the Turk. Lord Beaconsfield has told us that while the negotiations which ended in the Berlin Congress were going on, the Queen wrote to him every day, and telegraphed to him every hour, and this he said to Lady Bradford was a literal fact. But greatly as one must admire the courage, the clear decision, and the determination of the Queen to make England's power felt abroad, I cannot see that her vehement outpourings had any real effect upon the course of politics. Against the rock of Lord Derby's sullen impassivity the waves of royal wrath broke in vain. The Foreign Secretary stiffened his back, thrust out his under lip, and did nothing. Lord Beaconsfield, it is hardly necessary to say, was far too clever to go to war, when he could get what he wanted by threatening to go to war. At all periods of his life Disraeli was under the sway of feminine influence. When he was at the meridian of his career, driving Russia back from the gates of Constantinople, calling out the reserves, summoning black troops from India, and secretly acquiring Cyprus as a military station, he was in love with three women simultaneously, and all of them, as Schouveloff observed, grandmothers. It may well be that our Prime Minister persuaded himself that his Royal Mistress guided and inspired his foreign policy; but the world still smiles at the delusion.

In domestic politics the strong character and decided views of Queen Victoria naturally had greater influence, though not so much as we are asked to believe. It may surprise those who, like the late Lord Salisbury, were wont to abuse Disraeli for his " leap in the dark " in 1867, that the Franchise Bill was really forced upon the Conservative party by the Queen, who was determined that this matter, having been played with by many governments for so many years, should be settled. The Queen certainly interfered frequently and forcibly in the distribution of ecclesiastical patronage. She was decidedly Broad Church and would have liked to appoint nobody but Stanleys and Bradleys, which would have created an uproar. She despised the Low Church as " evangelical trash", and she roundly denounced the High Church party as Romanists in disguise. However, she prevented Disraeli from using Church appointments as a means of political influence.

Most of her critics miss the real greatness of Queen Victoria, which was neither political nor ecclesiastical, but social.

Insensibly, by no show of provincial puritanism, but by innate elevation of character, Victoria lifted the moral tone of England, and by mere simplicity contrived to surround reserve and dullness with the prestige of the eighteenth century. That she did it by herself is proved by the fact that her first mentors were an old *roué* and a German youth, who cannot have contributed to the result. The Queen made reception at her Court what she meant it to be, the recognition of rank, ability, and virtue.

On the subject of honours Queen Victoria entertained the strongest views, of which there are instances in her correspondence. She was pressed to confer a peerage on Chief Justice Cockburn, and refused because of his " notoriously bad moral character." Lord Granville answered jauntily, not to the Queen but to Sir Charles Phipps, that " Sir A. Cockburn was immoral as a young man in one line. He has two illegitimate children, and anyway he was no worse than Brougham or Lyndhurst."

Cockburn was told of the Queen's objection, and being unmarried gave up the idea of a peerage. Some years later, after the Alabama Arbitration, he was given the Grand Cross of the Bath.

An instance of Whiggish exclusiveness occurred when Disraeli went out of office in 1868, and when Victoria, who was really anxious to gratify him, asked what he wanted for himself. Disraeli asked that his wife should be made Viscountess Beaconsfield in her own right. The Queen was much embarrassed, and the Court thrown into giggles. We learn from General Grey that the hesitation was caused by a friendly fear lest the couple should become the object of endless ridicule. There you have the Whig point of view. Mrs. Disraeli a Viscountess, how absurd! Needless to say that when it was done, nobody saw anything ridiculous in it, and Lady Beaconsfield wrote the Queen a very pretty and dignified letter. It should also be remembered that General Grey had been Dizzy's successful opponent at Wycombe thirty-five years ago, and his memory was probably haunted by the vision of the Jew boy in pink waistcoat and velvet pantaloons, denouncing from the portico of the Red Lion Whigs in general and Greys and Caringtons in particular.

It was as a great lady who banished from the Court the horrors and scandals of her two predecessors, that Victoria deserves to be placed on a pedestal in history. Middle-class careerists and those who broke the marriage vow, were not received at Court, and would never have dreamed of attempting to get there. License, vulgarity and pretentiousness stood abashed in Queen Victoria's reign, and the subordination which is vital to the existence of society was preserved.

Disraeli's Meridian

DISRAELI'S MERIDIAN

EVEN middle-age cannot make Disraeli uninteresting, as all who have read Mr. Buckle's biography of him will agree. In a well-known passage of *Sibyl* Disraeli muses on the fact that there are certain historical personages over whom " a mysterious oblivion is encouraged to creep," and his instance of a " suppressed character " is Lord Shelburne. There seems no danger of oblivion creeping over Disraeli any more than over Samuel Johnson, or Buonaparte, or Chatham. Why are some individuals perennially interesting, while others, more powerful, perhaps, or more successful in their lives, fall into " the dusty crypt of darkened forms and faces " ? What are the qualities that arrest the attention of a man's contemporaries and of posterity ? Many poets, painters, philosophers, scientists are only discovered after death. It is different with statesmen and soldiers. But many party leaders, like the second Pitt, Peel, Gladstone, absorb public attention while they live, and after their death become mere names, pegs on which the historian hangs a tale. The striking thing about Disraeli is that, largely as he loomed in the eye of his contemporaries, the interest in his career and character grows stronger with the lapse of time. Has any other statesman been put upon the stage within thirty-five years of his death ? Yet in the middle of a fearful war people went to see the play, and read the book which Mr. Buckle has composed with so much dramatic skill and historical insight. What is the secret of Disraeli's posthumous popularity?

There are many reasons. Disraeli was the first purebred Hebrew who attained to supreme political power. There have been financial Jews ever since the world began—thousands of them—and there have been musical, artistic, literary Jews by the hundred. But never before did a Jew " break his birth's invidious bar " with such force as to rule a world-wide Empire. This is a point of great historical interest. In a letter to Mary Gladstone at the moment of Lord Beaconsfield's death Lord Acton wrote: " The *Pall Mall résumés* of Lord Beaconsfield have been intensely interesting. None seemed to me too severe, but some were shocking at the moment. He was quite remarkable enough to fill a column of Eloge. Some one wrote to me yesterday that no Jew for 1,800 years has played so great a part in the world. That would be no Jew since St. Paul; and it is very startling. But, putting aside literature, and, therefore, Spinoza and Heine, almost simultaneously with Disraeli, a converted Jew, Stahl, a man without birth or fortune, became the leader of the Prussian Conservative and aristocratic Party.

He led them from about 1850 to 1860, when he died; and he was intellectually far superior to Disraeli—I should say the greatest reasoner that has ever served the Conservative cause. But he never obtained power or determined any important event. Lassalle died after two years of agitation. Benjamin, the soul of the Confederate Ministry, now rising to the first rank of English lawyers, had too short and too disastrous a public career. In short, I have not yet found an answer." This is characteristic, for who but Lord Acton ever heard of Stahl? Another source of attraction was the unlikeness of Disraeli to everybody else—in appearance, manners, speech and thought. The nickname of "Old Oddity" gained a good deal of Dr. Johnson's celebrity. I was present at the debate in the House of Lords when Lord Beaconsfield explained the Treaty of Berlin.

" With grave
Aspect he rose, and in his rising seem'd
A pillar of State : deep on his front engraven
Deliberation sat, and public care."

He divided his speech into two parts, the first dealing with Europe, the second treating of the Eastern possessions of the Sultan. After dismissing the absurd pretensions of Greece with a counsel of patience, he stopped and put his hand into the inner breast-pocket of his frock-coat. He pulled out a tiny silver flask, deliberately unscrewed the top, took a pull at its contents, as deliberately replaced it, and turning to a grave and silent House said, " And now, my lords, I will ask you to accompany me into Asia." A wellbred ripple ran along the scarlet benches.

It was impossible not to be struck with his superiority to the surrounding peers. As he spoke, somehow or other, the Granvilles, the Derbys, and the Salisburys seemed to shrink into conventional mediocrities. Bagehot will have it that Disraeli's mind was intensely receptive of immediate impressions, but unoriginal, uncreative. Bagehot was fond of paradoxes, and this is one of his most foolish. The education of our public schools and universities has indisputable merits, but it has the fault of turning out its pupils in a conventional mould. Disraeli had not learned to speak at " Pop " or the Union ; he taught himself on the hustings and rehearsed in his father's library. It was his detachment from the vulgar prejudices of the upper and middle classes, his isolated and purely literary upbringing, that gave freshness and force to his speculations on politics.

A large number of persons in all Parties—Whigs, Tories, Radicals and " Gigadibs the literary man " ; Carlyle, Bagehot, Gladstone, Bright, Robert Cecil, Acton, Beresford Hope ; the *Saturday, Edinburgh* and *Quarterly Reviews* all combined to spread the legend that Disraeli was a wicked and immoral man. They shook their heads over his shiftiness, and gossiped about his debts. They could not have contributed more surely and effectively to the popular interest in his career. For who does not care more about Becky Sharp than about Amelia or Laura ? Thackeray intended that we should love Amelia and despise Becky. But Amelia and Laura are bores with their virtue and meekness, while we follow with the keenest interest, not always distinguishable from admiration, the turns and shifts and plots and combinations with which the dauntless Becky fought the world from the bandbox in Curzon Street. Nothing excites curiosity and sympathy so strongly as the suspicion of skeletons in the cupboard, of secret debts, of struggles behind the curtain. Gladstone was a pattern of propriety and prosperity. He never swore ; he shuddered at the smell of tobacco ; he frowned at a Rabelaisian anecdote ; he probably never had a debt in his life. That is why his biography, apart from his public transactions, is quite uninteresting, and will be read by nobody a hundred years hence. As for his superiority over his rival in the matter of unselfishness and public virtue, Mr. Buckle has effectively dispelled that legend.

It appears that not once, but twice or thrice, Disraeli offered to give up to Gladstone the lead of the House of Commons if he would join the Conservative Party, which at that time he supported by his voice and pen. The celebrated letter is too long to quote, but I believe everyone will admit that it is a model of manly self-effacement and chivalrous obeisance to a rival. It made no impression on Gladstone ; he had other and longer views ; he was far too astute to be touched by his rival's generous impulse ; he coldly declined Disraeli's offer. If there was one man whom Gladstone abused in private and resolutely opposed in public it was Lord Palmerston. In 1859 Gladstone supported Lord Derby's Government against the vote of want of confidence, and a few weeks later accepted the post of Chancellor of the Exchequer in Palmerston's Government. The reason was plain. Palmerston was verging on his eightieth year ; Russell was nearly as old ; Gladstone saw that if he joined the Liberals he *must* succeed to the leadership, and so he joined them. And yet Gladstone was regarded by his contemporaries as a pattern of public virtue, while Disraeli was treated to " thimble-rigger," " conjurer," " charlatan," " self-seeking adventurer."

We see these things more clearly now, and Disraeli gains much by the contrast with the unctuous rectitude of his great opponent. The crowning quality of Disraeli's attractiveness was his wit. " With words," said Mephistopheles to Faust, " you can do everything " ; and certainly Disraeli's power over the English language is only comparable to Byron's. England, like all democracies, is governed by words ; but witty words have always been rare, and seem nowadays to have disappeared. Gladstone governed by words, as did Asquith, but in neither was there a spark of wit or humour ; and even the Irish have grown dull. For sheer wit and irresistible drollery, Disraeli's speech at Slough on the collapse of Cardwell's vote of censure cannot be beaten, and has never even been approached in political literature. Who could be long or seriously angry with a man who rejoiced, in the heat of the Reform battle, that " a good broad piece of furniture separated him from Gladstone " ; who described Lord Shaftesbury as

"Gamaliel himself with the broad phylacteries of faction on his forehead"; who spoke of "the stately cynicism" of Sir James Graham and "the Batavian grace" of Mr. Beresford Hope; who pictured the Treasury bench as "a row of extinct volcanoes"; and who dismissed Peel's hackneyed quotations with the remark that "they were the better appreciated because most of them had already received the meed of Parliamentary approbation."

The pregnant lesson which Disraeli's meridian should convey to the present generation is the value, or, rather, the necessity, of a powerful leader of the Opposition. Three-fourths of Disraeli's life were spent in the position in which, as Mr. Buckle teaches us by inexpugnable records, he shared the cares, though not the cash or the credit, of Government. This unfair partition of rewards and punishments was not of Disraeli's choosing, though he saw clearly the reason of it. Palmerston was a Conservative in the skin of a Liberal. The middle class, then the rulers of England, knew this, and were content that Palmerston should check the Radicals, and that Disraeli should check Palmerston and Russell in their foreign policy. Lord Derby also knew it, and with his racing and his Lancashire rents in his pocket, was content to visit the House of Lords between his fits of gout and fire an occasional broadside into "old Pam." But Disraeli was naturally far from contented, as is shown by the following passage from a draft letter to Horsman, written in 1859, just before the fall of the second Derby

Administration: "If the usual combination throws us out, Lord Palmerston is to be the next man, and will form a Government with his friends, and is to be supported, not generally, but invaryingly, by mine sitting opposite to him. I have no doubt he will govern the country well, but I do not see why he should do it better than us, nor do I see why this hocus-pocus should be perpetually repeated." It was to avoid the impending fate of this perpetual hocus-pocus that Disraeli made such frantic attempts to get Graham, Gladstone, or Palmerston to join forces with him. "Dis aliter visum": it was not to be. Of Disraeli's controlling influence over the foreign policy of the country from the Opposition bench there are proofs on every page of history. Disraeli was the first statesman to establish the patriotic doctrine, that it is the duty of an Opposition to support the Government in the prosecution of a war, provided the Government does prosecute it earnestly. He took no party advantage of Roebuck's Committee to inquire into the scandalous mismanagement of the Crimean War. But as soon as he saw that there was nothing more to be gained by the war, he pressed the Government, in the teeth of a bellicose Press and angry public, to make an early peace, as they did. The Indian Mutiny broke out under Palmerston's Government, which followed the Aberdeen Coalition. With a prescience, as rare as the courage by which it was supported, Disraeli set himself against the policy of vindictiveness, which the massacre of Cawnpore and the siege of Lucknow and Delhi excited in this country. Luckily, on the sudden expulsion of Palmerston from office by the French colonels, the settlement of India fell into the hands of the Derby Government. Disraeli, in a minority of the House of Commons, after literally laughing Palmerston and his satellites out of court, modified Lord Canning's policy of confiscation in Oude, and transferred the Government of India from " John Company " to the Secretary of State in Council. When we read Bagehot's sneer at Disraeli's constructive capacity, and remember his epigram that " Disraeli's chaff was exquisite, but his wheat was poor stuff," let us correct it by remembering that in a brief year's tenure of office without a majority Disraeli created the system by which our Indian Empire is governed at this hour. Before passing from this topic of Disraeli's creative or legislative power, let me add that in 1867, when Disraeli was in office for two years and a half, again without a majority, he placed upon the Statute Book the British North America Act, which provided the Dominion of Canada with the charter of its liberty and progress. It is literal truth to say that in three years, while wrestling with a factious majority, Disraeli did more for the British Empire than Palmerston and Gladstone achieved in fifty years, supported as they were by a complaisant Press and their well-disciplined battalions in the House of Commons. Over the reckless and often ridiculous European policy of Russell and Palmerston a very salutary control was exercised by Disraeli. An alliance with France was, as Mr. Buckle says, the root of Disraeli's foreign policy; but in his desire to forward it he took a perfectly unpardonable step in 1859. Disraeli had not a high idea of the ability of Lord Cowley; he thought that he was not as alert and well-informed as an Ambassador ought to be, and (still worse) that he was not on good terms with the French emperor. He despatched his private secretary, Mr. Ralph Earle—"*infelix puer atque impar congressus Achilli*"—on a secret mission to Paris to pump, if possible, Napoleon III. France was on the brink of that short war with Austria which restored Lombardy to Italy, and it was essential that the British Government should have first-hand information. The mission was a failure, for Napoleon was quite as sphinx-like as Disraeli, and declined to be pumped by an audacious boy of twenty-three. But the impropriety of Disraeli's conduct is obvious, and his only excuse is that his Foreign Secretary, Lord Malmesbury, was indolent and incompetent, and that his Ambassador was not at the centre of things in Paris. Still, our diplomacy would be ten times more dangerous than it is if the Prime Minister or the Chancellor of the Exchequer were to communicate with foreign Powers by his private secretary without the knowledge of the Secretary of State or the Ambassador. Yet you never can tell. What might have happened if Mr. Asquith had secretly despatched Mr. Bonham Carter to talk to the Kaiser in 1914 without telling Sir Edward Grey or Sir Edward Goschen? What, indeed? Whatever might have happened, it could not have been worse than what did happen.

It was chiefly in regard to British policy towards Austria, Prussia, and Russia that Disraeli's steadying influence was felt. Two more perfectly reckless old men than Palmerston and Russell probably never governed Great Britain. Palmerston, who never lifted a finger to help the cause of Liberalism at home —who, indeed, devoted his masterly inactivity to blocking Parliamentary reform—was very fond of lecturing the absolute Monarchies of Europe about liberty. Palmerston and Russell wrote and talked as if they were prepared to go to war with Russia for the emancipation of Poland, with Austria for the restoration of Venetia, and with Prussia and Austria for the protection of Denmark in her defence of the Duchies. Disraeli pointed out that to interfere with the affairs of great Continental Monarchies, unless you are prepared to back your interference with armies, is to court rebuffs and humiliation. He knew that England was not prepared to embark on a second European war within a few years of the Crimean War and the Indian Mutiny. He believed that such a war might range France against us; and with the secret assistance of the Court he succeeded in preventing the Government from plunging us into a policy of adventures for which we were not armed.

Against the snubs and buffets which rained upon Lord John Russell from the Courts of St. Petersburg, Berlin and Paris, the leader of the Opposition was not concerned to protect him. The prestige of England on the Continent sank very low in these years, though it must remain a disputed point whether it was Queen Victoria who, at the eleventh hour, prevented the Government from going to war with Prussia and Austria in defence of Denmark.

The letters which passed between the Queen and Disraeli show us the secret of the statesman's success as a courtier. Disraeli's insight into the foibles of the men and women with whom he had to deal was almost "diabolical," to use Gladstone's favourite epithet. After a visit to Woburn he thus characterises one of the phalanx of Whig houses: "The predominant feature and organic deficiency of the Russell family is shyness. Even Hastings" (afterwards the ninth Duke of Bedford) "is not free from it, though he struggles to cover it with an air of uneasy gaiety." He perceived that the ruling passion of Queen Victoria was her love of her husband. I do not accuse Disraeli of exploiting this sentiment for his own ends. Doubtless he did appreciate Prince Albert, who was a clever and well-educated German. But Disraeli was forced to win allies where he could, and perhaps to gain the confidence of the Sovereign, he played a little upon the emotions of the widow. What else can explain the outrageous nonsense of the letter he wrote to the Queen in 1863 just after the Prince Consort's death? "The Prince is the only person whom Mr. Disraeli has ever known who realised the ideal. None with whom he is acquainted has ever approached it.

There was in him a union of the manly grace and sublime simplicity, of chivalry with the intellectual splendour of the Attic Academe. The only character in English history that would, in some respects, draw near to him is Sir Philip Sidney," etc. Of course, the Prince Consort was no more like Sir Philip Sidney than he was like the Black Prince. What Mr. Buckle gently calls " this somewhat hyperbolic eulogium " had its reward. A somewhat similar feeling of repugnance is aroused in my mind by Disraeli's speeches on the Church and his attendance at diocesan meetings. I feel inclined to say " hear, hear " to the curt entry in Bishop Wilberforce's diary after listening to one of Disraeli's performances on the religious trombone— " a clever electioneering speech."

Disraeli's career reached its zenith with his great personal triumph in 1867, and his accession to the Premiership on the retirement of Lord Derby in 1868. With regard to the once vexed question of Parliamentary reform, Disraeli was neither better nor worse than his opponents. It is impossible to read the insincere manœuvres of the two Parties on the extension of the franchise without thinking of what Halifax said of the quarrels of Whigs and Tories in the seventeenth century about religion—" it is like two men quarrelling about a woman for whom neither cares a pin." As Bulwer Lytton said of the Reform Bill of 1859 : " Nine out of ten said loudly ' We must have a Reform Bill ' ; but eight out of every nine whispered to each other, ' Does anybody want one ?' "

Palmerston certainly did not, and though he allowed Russell to bring in three Bills, he allowed each of them to be rejected. Disraeli, of course, saw that if he suffered the Liberal Party to establish a monopoly of Parliamentary Reform, he might as well retire from politics and leave his Party to disappear as completely as the Tories disappeared for fifty-five years after Bolingbroke's flight in 1715. He accordingly brought in two Bills, which the Liberals threw out. Such was the state of the Reform question when Palmerston's death in 1865 removed the real obstruction. Then the game began in earnest. Gladstone, the ex-Tory, brought in his Bill in 1866 for lowering the Borough franchise to £7 rental. Disraeli defeated this Bill by splitting up the Liberal majority of seventy, and took Gladstone's place as Chancellor of the Exchequer. The prime movers of the Reform Bill of 1867 were the Queen and Lord Derby, while Disraeli, having just won a great battle, was disposed to rest his weary limbs in " the warm precincts of the Treasury." But the Queen was insistent to have this great question settled ; she pressed Lord Derby, who pressed the war-worn Disraeli. Such was the genesis of " the leap in the dark," the great Tory-Radical Reform Act which swept away all rental qualifications and introduced bare household franchise. It has been argued that the result of the Reform Act of 1867 was to place the Conservatives in power for twenty-four out of forty-eight years. It is a shallow observation. It was not household suffrage but Parnell who gave Lord

Salisbury and Mr. Balfour eighteen years of office. The Queen purred and Lord Derby chuckled over "the dishing of the Whigs." What did Disraeli himself think? Disraeli was remarkably tenacious of his ideas. In *The Spirit of Whiggism*, written in 1836, Disraeli had argued that we never would have democracy in this country, no matter how extended the suffrage, so long as the distribution of property was unaltered, and the distribution of property would never be altered by a people who worshipped wealth and reverenced law. We know better to-day; but Disraeli could not foresee the Finance Act of 1909, or the Great War. In 1867 he doubtless thought that household suffrage was a safe experiment. However we may differ about democracy, we must all " pursue the triumph and partake the gale " of this extraordinary life. We leave Disraeli in the meridian of his career, toasted amidst the frantic cheers of the Carlton Club, welcomed—which he valued more—by the ecstasy of his devoted wife, and promoted by a smiling Sovereign to the highest honour a subject can enjoy.

Ten years later Lord Beaconsfield, "the centre of the world's desire," was Prime Minister, not alone of England, but of Europe. When he returned from Berlin and drove through cheering crowds to Downing Street, his mind must have jumped the half-century and dwelt on his first novel, *Vivian Grey*, and his first speech in Parliament, "I have begun many things, and have often failed, but I have always succeeded at last."

The Marquis of Salisbury

THE EARL OF BEACONSFIELD
From Vanity Fair

THE MARQUIS OF SALISBURY

LORD SALISBURY's life divides itself into three chapters. There was the period between 1853 and 1866, when Lord Robert Cecil was a younger son living with his wife and family on an allowance from his father and what he earned by writing articles in the *Quarterly* and *Saturday Reviews*. This was the bitter and rebellious period. There was the period between 1866 and 1881, when after the death of his brother and father, he bloomed into the Marquisate, a large rent roll, and the occupancy of Hatfield. During the last four years of this mellowing time he became Secretary for Foreign Affairs, and Lord Beaconsfield's first lieutenant. There was the final phase, from Disraeli's death in 1881 to his own death in 1903. He became Leader of the Tory Party, and formed four Administrations in '85, '86, '95, and 1900.

The *Life of Lord Salisbury** by Lady Gwendolen Cecil, is, I believe the first attempt by a woman to write a biography on a big scale. It is natural, and perhaps proper, for his daughter to think that Lord Salisbury was a greater man than Lord Beaconsfield; that Lord Cranborne was right and Disraeli wrong in the quarrels over the Reform Bill of 1867; and that it was the Foreign Secretary, not the Prime Minister,

**Life of the Marquis of Salisbury*, by Lady Gwendolen Cecil. 2 Vols. Hodder and Stoughton, 1921.

who made the Berlin Congress a success. Lady Gwendolen is perfectly entitled to hold these views; but the world has long ago decided against them; and her determination to force them upon her readers is often wearisome, and sometimes absurd. Lord Beaconsfield has been dead forty-six years; three biographies have appeared in the last six months and there is hardly a page of political writing on which his sayings are not quoted.

Lord Robert Cecil's boyhood and early youth are a dismal tale of ill-health and morbid egotism. He was bullied at school—as a boy will be who won't play games, who can't keep his hat on his head, or his clothes clean, and who gives no sign of intellectual precocity. He was obliged on the score of health to leave Christ Church after two years with what amounted to an honorary degree; and his beginning of life was a kind of hymn of hate. He hated his preparatory school; he hated Eton; he hated the Peerage and the Court Guide; and worst of all he hated Mr. Disraeli, fifteen years his senior, and the acknowledged leader of his Party. What are we to say to a young man who, born in the purple, tells his father at the age of twenty-six: "I do not enjoy anything. Amusements I have none"? His father, who apparently wished to provide him with some occupation, offered him a colonelcy in the Middlesex Militia, to which Lord Robert replied, "Your proposition gave me a stomach ache all this morning." Such morbidity is pathetic; but, although physically handicapped, he had no lack of moral courage. With £300 a year from his mother, and £100 a year from his father (not a very magnificent allowance from the Marquis of Salisbury to his son), Lord Robert Cecil married Miss Alderson with £100 a year of her own, and took a house in Fitzroy Square. In the middle of last century £500 a year was about the equivalent of £1,000 to-day; but for a young Lord, born and bred at Hatfield, it was little enough wherewith to start married life. I doubt if Lord Robert ever made more than £300 or £400 a year by his pen. Four articles in the *Quarterly Review* would mean £160 by the tariff then ruling; he could not have made more than £200 a year out of the *Saturday Review*, even though it was run by his millionaire brother-in-law, Mr. James Beresford Hope, for the editor, J. D. Cook, did not always accept his articles, and sometimes kept them on hand for a longer time than a needy contributor likes. Putting all these things together, the Robert Cecils could not have had a larger income than £800 or £900; and one cannot help wondering what would have happened to the future Prime Minister if his elder brother had not died some ten years later.

I protest against the assumption of moral superiority that pervades the portion of the biography devoted to Lord Salisbury's career as journalist and Member of Parliament from 1853 to 1868. For this Olympian attitude there is, on the facts, no warrant. What are the facts? In 1853 Lord Exeter popped Lord Robert Cecil in for Stamford, one of the small boroughs that escaped the scythe of the first Reform Act, and still remained in the pocket of a great family. For fifteen years Lord Robert was returned without a contest, which was really a misfortune : if he had been obliged to fight two or three contested elections he might have gained some knowledge of the character of *l'homme moyen sensuel*, who always was a perfect stranger to Lord Salisbury. During those fifteen years Lord Robert persistently and virulently attacked Disraeli in the *Saturday Review*, in the *Quarterly Review*, and in *Bentley's Quarterly Review*. It was not surprising that Lord Exeter, who supplied the seat, and Lord Salisbury (the father), who paid the bills, should have remonstrated with this very independent Member. Lord Robert Cecil's reply was that he voted with the party because by not doing so he might injure it—as if his writings in the Press did the party no injury ! To Lord Exeter he explained more particularly that Disraeli was Lord Derby's lieutenant, and that it was the Derby Government that he supported. As Disraeli was leader of the party in the House of Commons this was a very flimsy excuse. To his father, however, he gave another explanation. Disraeli was a personal friend of Lord Salisbury, who constantly received him at Hatfield, and who had accepted a post in the Tory Government of 1859. Naturally Lord Salisbury told his son that he objected not only to these anonymous attacks, but to the indecorous language in which they were couched. Lord Robert replied thus : " It must be remembered that I write for money . . . I must therefore write so as best to gain money . . . What I do write I must write in a style that is most likely to attract, and therefore sell." And Lady Gwendolen harps on the cynicism of Lord Derby and Disraeli! I don't know how it may have been in the early Victorian era; but in the 'eighties, when I was in Parliament, and Lord Salisbury was Premier, a Conservative member who was known to attack his leader anonymously in the papers, and did so regularly for a livelihood, would have had a rough time in the lobbies and smoking rooms. I should have thought that there could be no two opinions about such conduct. The case is aggravated by the fact that Disraeli always went out of his way to be courteous and encouraging to the young Member. Disraeli knew that his friend's son was persistently attacking him under the veil of anonymity, for Disraeli had been a journalist himself, and was perfectly informed as to what was going on in that world; yet in the Government formed by himself and Derby in 1866, Lord Cranborne, as the Member for Stamford had become by the death of his brother, was offered and accepted the coveted post of Secretary of State for India. Such magnanimity is very rare in party politics, and might have placated its object. On the contrary, within a few months Lord Cranborne renewed his attacks upon the Leader of the House of Commons, both on the floor and in the Press, with increased venom. Now what are the facts about the Reform Bill of 1867? After the death of Lord Palmerston in 1866, Gladstone introduced a Reform Bill to lower the franchise in boroughs from £10 to £7 rental and in the counties from £50 to £14. The Whigs thought the Bill went too far; the Radicals thought it did not go far enough; the Tories thought that it was the business of the Opposition to oppose. Between these forces Gladstone fell in the summer of 1866, and Lord Derby was invited by the Queen to form a Government in a Parliament with a hostile majority. Lord Derby might, of course, have dissolved; but besides the fact that there had been a General Election the year before, men of all parties, Whigs, Tories, and Radicals, had time to reflect upon the situation. We had not yet got compulsory gratuitous education; but the artisans in the towns were beginning to educate themselves and their children by attendance at lectures and evening classes at the institutes. The writings of Darwin, Huxley and Tyndall were abroad, and permeating the mind of the nation. It really was impossible for any House of Commons to postpone or trifle with the extension of the franchise. Indeed, Lady Gwendolen herself, in one of the happiest phrases of her book, explains Disraeli's almost magical success in passing his Reform Bill as " the avenging power of fact over the self-created delusions of politicians." The first person to perceive the realities of the situation was Queen Victoria. After turning Gladstone out, Disraeli was inclined to rest on his oars, while Lord Derby was, as usual, only too delighted to read racing results instead of Parliamentary debates. But the Queen was a serious and resolute woman; and she wrote a long letter to Lord Derby insisting that his Government should settle without delay the question of Parliamentary reform. This letter was written in October, '66, and must have been communicated to the November Cabinet which Lord Cranborne attended. All through December the discussion was continued in the Cabinet, and it was decided to proceed by tabling resolutions instead of introducing a Bill. That was purely a question of method, not of principle; and it was soon abandoned for a Bill. This change was denounced by Lord Cranborne as a species of political crime. The short time given to drafting the clauses of the Bill was regarded by General Peel, Lord Cranborne, and Lord Carnarvon as political profligacy so dangerous that they all resigned from the Cabinet at a peculiarly critical moment in February. General Peel one can forgive; he was avenging his father. But what is to be said for Lords Cranborne and Carnarvon? The subject of Parliamentary reform had been steadily discussed for the past twenty years, and at least two Reform Bills had been introduced during Lord Cranborne's membership of the House of Commons. There was not a detail, not a clause, not a schedule, in any possible Reform Bill that was not perfectly familiar to every member on both sides of the House. Disraeli took his stand upon " the avenging power of fact " over party politics. He assumed as his major premiss that, in the interest of the House of Commons as well as of the nation, the question of lowering the franchise had to be settled then and there, by and with the consent of all parties. Granting this assumption, in which the Sovereign, and all his colleagues, with three exceptions, concurred, there was no question of principle involved; it was merely a matter of detail, of clauses and schedules. As the measure was to be passed with the co-operation of the whole House, it followed that the details had to be changed from time to time to secure acceptance by the different groups. Lady Gwendolen, with acid contempt, brands this policy as " pure opportunism." Of course it was; but opportunism is sometimes the highest wisdom. We shall find plenty of pure opportunism when we come to the Tory Governments of '85 and '86, and see Lord Carnarvon—who is exhibited to us in these pages as a Paladin of politics, the soul of honour and chivalry, shuddering at the pliability of Disraeli—as Viceroy of Ireland, twittering in the twilight of Parnellism.

Abstractedly and theoretically, I agree with Robert Lowe and Robert Cecil in their denunciations of the dangers of democracy, for I regard a Government founded on universal suffrage as a self-cancelling business, which ends in zero. When one-twentieth of the nation pays five-sixths of the taxes, the result must sooner or later end in a Dictatorship. But speeches in the House and essays in the *Quarterly Review* will not make people believe this conclusion; the Dictator will come with the avenging power of fact in his hand. His appearance is still a long way off, and meanwhile who does not see that the superior morality of Lords Cranborne and Carnarvon had no place either in ethics or in practical politics? I fail to perceive Disraeli's wickedness because, distinguishing essentials from unessentials, he refused to be tragical over the difference between a £7 rental and a £5 rating, or between a £5 rating and residential suffrage. A generation which has witnessed the enfranchisement of twelve million voters of both sexes, after a few nights' perfunctory debate, will dismiss with a tolerant smile or an impatient shrug the furious futilities of Lords Cranborne and Carnarvon.

When the Bill was passed, Lord Derby retired on the ground of ill-health, and Disraeli became Prime Minister in 1868. As the custom is, he was obliged to reconstruct his Government. With that absence of vindictiveness which marked his character, and which, I think, placed him on a higher moral plane than those who attacked him, Disraeli sent Sir Stafford Northcote to find out whether, now that the Reform question was out of the way, Lord Cranborne would rejoin the Cabinet. The answer was reported by himself in a letter to Lord Carnarvon. " I told him I had a great respect for every member of the Government except one—but that I did not think my honour was safe in the hands of that one." The wanton insolence and bad feeling of this reply can only be realised if we remember that the leading members of the Government were Cairns, Richmond, Stanley, Gathorne

Hardy, and Stafford Northcote, who had all marched step by step with their Chief through the " Great Surrender." Lady Gwendolen surmises that " as Sir Stafford Northcote was eminently a man of peace," he did not transmit this message to his Chief. I should base my surmise on the fact that Sir Stafford Northcote was a gentleman.

In 1868, on his father's death, Lord Cranborne was translated from Duchess Street to Hatfield and Arlington Street, with a handsome rent-roll from London and Herts. Characteristically, the new Marquis of Salisbury opens a black suit. He groans over the burthen of estate management, and laments the boredom of hospitality. Nevertheless, the man was much improved by affluence and a peerage; he would have been more or less than human if he had not been. Lord Salisbury's temper, soured, no doubt, by early struggles with impecuniosity, was softened; his latent sense of humour was aroused; and something very like geniality took the place of austerity. After six years of Gladstone's plundering and blundering, Disraeli found himself for the first time in his life, able to form a Government with a substantial majority. It was impossible, even for Disraeli, to forget the insult of 1868; and it was therefore necessary to find an honest broker if Lord Salisbury was to join the Cabinet of 1874. The intermediary appeared in the person of " My Lady," Lord Salisbury's stepmother, then the wife of Lord Derby, the " young Morose " of Disraeli's early days. She succeeded in starting a correspondence between "My dear Lord" and "Dear Mr. Disraeli," which ended in Lord Salisbury returning to the India Office. The relations between the two men improved rapidly from that date, although the confidence and admiration which the older man extended to the younger were never quite reciprocated. Indeed, in one of the letters written by Lord Salisbury to his wife from the Berlin Congress, it is rather amusing to find that the Cecil family evidently regarded Lord Beaconsfield as a pottering figurehead, the success of the business being, of course, due to his lieutenant. On June 23rd, 1878, Lord Salisbury writes : " There is no news since I wrote yesterday—except that my Chief is distressing himself very much about the supposed designs of Bismarck ; what with deafness, ignorance of French, and Bismarck's extraordinary mode of speech, Beaconsfield has not the dimmest idea of what is going on—understands everything crossways—and imagines a perpetual conspiracy." I believe the second lion always thinks the first a bore.

" The greatest of British interests is peace," is a maxim only true if it be remembered that a nation may pay too high a price for peace. Lord Salisbury preserved peace in Europe whilst he lived. The question is whether his foreign policy did not lead inevitably to the Great War in 1914. The author of the saying just quoted was Lord Derby, who never said a foolish thing and seldom did a wise one. If his cold nature ever felt anything like affection and admiration for any public man it was for Lord Beaconsfield, who made him Foreign Secretary in the Cabinet of 1874. Yet he deserted his leader in 1878 because Lord Beaconsfield stopped Russia at the gates of Constantinople by despatching the Fleet to the Dardanelles and calling Indian troops to Malta. Lord Salisbury had at last recognized the commanding personality, which he had so long resisted. He succeeded Lord Derby at the Foreign Office, and " the master of flouts and gibes " had no words too strong to condemn the impotent pacifism of his late colleague.

He compared Lord Derby's explanation to the discoveries of Titus Oates, and summed up his character in one of the wittiest and bitterest epigrams in the range of political invective. " My noble friend," he said, " will never stray far from the frontier lines of either party, and he reserves all his powers of being disagreeable for those with whom he is temporarily associated." The action from which Lord Derby shrank, with the flawless logic of a pacifist, forced Russia to submit the treaty which had been wrung from Turkey at San Stefano to the arbitrament of the European Powers, who saved Constantinople by the Treaty of Berlin. Would that Lord Salisbury had adhered to the Eastern policy of Disraeli! No sooner had the election of 1880 removed Lord Beaconsfield from power than Gladstone began the reversal of his rival's foreign policy. Indeed, he could hardly avoid doing so, seeing that the Bulgarian atrocities campaign of 1877 and the Midlothian campaign of 1880 consisted of nothing but denunciations of "the unspeakable Turk" and the Minister who had protected him. At the opening of Parliament in 1881 Lord Beaconsfield complained that, in defiance of the tradition of continuity of policy, the new Government had given the order for "perpetual and complete reversal of all that had occurred" in foreign, Colonial, and Irish affairs. That the Liberal party should have so acted was bad enough; but that Lord Salisbury should have been induced to abandon Lord Beaconsfield's policy of supporting the Sultan for the policy, partly religious, partly philanthropic, and wholly sentimental, of patronising the Balkan States, was deplorable; and exactly the consequences predicted by Lord Beaconsfield ensued in the following thirty years. Lord Beaconsfield's policy of maintaining the independence and territorial integrity of Turkey was no sentimental predilection of a Jew for his cousins of the Koran; it was a clear perception of the realities of world politics, supplemented by a profound knowledge of human nature. In July, 1878, Lords Beaconsfield and Salisbury returned from Berlin and drove in triumph from Charing Cross to Downing Street, bringing peace with honour. A few days later the Prime Minister expounded his Eastern policy to a crowded House of Lords. "Her Majesty's Government at all times have resisted the partition of Turkey," said Lord Beaconsfield. "They have done so because, apart from the high-moral considerations that are mixed up with the subject, they believed an attempt, on a great scale, to accomplish the partition of Turkey would inevitably lead to a long, a sanguinary, and often recurring struggle, and that Europe and Asia would both be involved in a series of troubles and sources of disaster and danger of which no adequate idea could be formed." We know in 1927 the troubles, disasters and dangers in which Europe and Asia have been involved by the attempt to partition Turkey. But in 1878 Disraeli foresaw that if the Balkan States were encouraged by Russia, or the Western Powers, to attack Turkey, and if British support were withdrawn from Constantinople, the following results would ensue: (1) The Balkan States would quarrel over the spoils and would attack one another: (2) Russia and Austria, the two competitors for the Protectorate or Suzerainty of Eastern Europe, would be obliged to intervene, and ultimately to go to war with one another; (3) war between Austria and Russia would mean a world-war; (4) war against Turkey would create disaffection, if not rebellion, among the Mahommedan subjects of Britain in India; (5) if Britain ceased to be the predominant Power at Constantinople, some other Great Power would step into her shoes, to the peril of the British Empire. All these consequences have exactly followed from the pro-Balkan and anti-Turkish policy adopted by both Liberal and Conservative Governments since 1881. Lord Salisbury saw eye to eye with Lord Beaconsfield in 1878. How are we to account for his recidivism after his leader's death? His daughter tells us (Vol. II,

p. 326) that when he went back to the Foreign Office in 1885, one of his earliest inquiries of its documents was as to the actual condition of our influence at Constantinople. He returned from the investigation in despair. "They have just thrown it away into the sea," he exclaimed, "without getting anything whatever in exchange." But Lord Salisbury was in office from '85 until 1902, with the exception of the three years between '92 and '95, when Lord Rosebery, who agreed with his Foreign policy, was Secretary of State. Are we then to understand that in these seventeen years Lords Salisbury and Rosebery failed to recover the influence at Constantinople which Gladstone and Granville had thrown away? That seems an impossible explanation, especially if we remember that Lord Salisbury referred to the Treaties of Paris and Berlin as a mistake, or rather a miscalculation. Without perhaps realizing it, he did slip back into a Liberal Eastern policy, and even boasted of it. "We put our money on the wrong horse," said Lord Salisbury. Indeed no! Palmerston and Disraeli did not back the wrong horse. Let us see how Disraeli's prophecy was fulfilled. In 1912 Bulgaria, Serbia, and Greece attacked Turkey, beat her (despite of assistance from Germany in the shape of officers and munitions), and took territory from her. That was the first Balkan war. In 1913 Bulgaria, dissatisfied with its share of the plunder, attacked Serbia, Roumania, and Greece. That was the second Balkan war, intently watched by Russia and Austria. In 1914 Austria, now thoroughly alarmed by the growth of Slavia, seized the pretext of the Archduke's murder to declare war on Serbia, and in the Great War which followed Turkey appeared as the vassal of Germany, bound by a treaty made under the nose of the British Ambassador at Constantinople. Such were the results of a foreign policy in Eastern Europe based on religious prejudice and humanitarian sentiment. For I can find no other reasons for backing the Balkan States against the Sultan. During the factious agitation in 1877 started by Mr. Gladstone in favour of Bulgaria, his family and followers were in the habit of referring to themselves (with that lack of humour which dogged the conduct of their Chief) as " we Christians." The spirit of the Crusaders is still discernible in Lord Salisbury's family; and I have often been struck by the stream of sympathy between the houses of Gladstone and Cecil.

No doubt, *idem sentire de ecclesiâ* is a strong bond of social friendship; but it is no foundation for a national policy. We know more about the Christians of Eastern Europe than we did before the war. And ruffian as the Turk has proved himself to be, we know now that, judged by our standards of civilization, there is between Turk and Bulgar and Serb and Greek not a pin to choose. Of course Lord Grey must share with Mr. Gladstone and Lord Salisbury the blame for the anti-British pro-Balkan policy.

The one saying of Lord Beaconsfield quoted in these pages without a sneer is the remark made to the author that Lord Salisbury was the only man of real courage with whom he had ever worked. It pains me to say on closing the book that Lady Gwendolen Cecil seems from first to last untouched by the genius and generosity of the great statesman who was so kind to her father, and to whom her father was so unkind.

The ancients, with true philosophic instinct, refused to pronounce any man happy until he was dead. Lord Salisbury ended a great and busy life more happily, it seems to me, than any of his predecessors, except perhaps Lord Palmerston. He alone, true to the Ha! ha! style until his death, passed peacefully away in actual possession of the symbols of authority, if not of governing power. When Lord Salisbury retired in 1902 he was the benevolent despot of a united Party, which was more powerful in Parliament and in the constituencies than any British Party had ever been before. He enjoyed in unstinted measure the confidence of his Sovereign; and he was, unquestionably, the most influential statesman in the world. What more could the heart of man desire? There is something more which the heart of every good man desires, and that was given to Lord Salisbury. He saw the growing success of those who were near to him, whom he wished to please, and whom he loved. His eldest son (Lord Cranborne) was Under Secretary of State for Foreign Affairs. Another of his sons (Lord Hugh Cecil) was acknowledged to be amongst the most brilliant orators in the House of Commons.

Another (Lord Edward) had distinguished himself as an officer in the South African War; while yet another (Lord Robert) was enjoying a lucrative practice at the Parliamentary bar. One of his daughters was married to a young statesman (Lord Selborne) of blameless reputation and occupant of the post of First Lord of the Admiralty. One of his nephews was First Lord of the Treasury (Mr. Arthur Balfour), Leader of the House of Commons, and his uncle's inevitable successor. Another nephew (Mr. Gerald Balfour) was President of the Board of Trade, and a sister's daughter was married to the Chairman of Ways and Means (Mr. J. W. Lowther). Surely no statesman was ever so happy in his public and private life as Lord Salisbury.

It is remarkable that Lord Salisbury never really had a rival, in the sense of a contemporary competitor for power, either on his own side or the opposite. Gladstone and Disraeli, who were much of an age, were his seniors by about fifteen years, and belonged to a previous generation. Nevertheless, Lord Salisbury made more than one attempt to throw the adventurous genius, whom he secretly disliked with the *morgue* of a great English noble. But Disraeli was too much for him, and during the lifetime of that dominating personality, Lord Salisbury was obliged to play second fiddle. Competitors for the first place he had none, for the Gathorne Hardys and Stafford Northcotes belonged to a different category of men. The fifteenth Lord Derby at one time threatened him as a possible successor to Disraeli; but Lord Derby was cursed with the judicial mind; and his retirement from Lord Beaconsfield's Ministry in 1878, upon the calling out of the reserves, and his subsequent acceptance of office from Mr. Gladstone, made Lord Salisbury's succession secure. When Lord Beaconsfield died, Lord Salisbury found himself confronted for a short time by Mr. Gladstone, who had enjoyed in the country a power immeasurably greater than his own. It is more than doubtful whether Lord Salisbury could have defeated Home Rule without the assistance of Lord Hartington and Mr. Chamberlain. However, that assistance he obtained, and on the ruins of the Liberal Party he rose to the ascendancy in his own country and the outer world which he claimed and kept from 1886 until 1902.

On Mr. Gladstone's retirement in 1894, Lord Salisbury's position can only be compared to that of the second Pitt; he was on a pedestal apart; there was no one near him. To Lord Kimberley, the titular leader of the House of Lords, he extended the grave courtesy due to official position and respectability. Lord Rosebery he always treated as the spoilt and brilliant boy whose exuberant declamation was to be smiled at rather than answered. It was a misfortune for Lord Salisbury that he was not confronted by a rival of his own age, by a foeman worthy of his steel. Every man requires a whetstone, and latterly Lord Salisbury became sluggish, and too indifferent to the man in the street.

How did Lord Salisbury achieve the position of one of the most powerful Premiers that ever ruled the British Empire? By the old, though always rare, qualities of industry, courage, and rectitude of character. He had high rank and considerable wealth, which helped him much. What would have become of Lord Robert Cecil, had his elder brother lived, it is idle to speculate. But other Prime Ministers have had rank and wealth, Lord Rockingham and the Duke of Portland, for instance, who have passed quickly across the stage leaving no memory behind them. It was not his marquisate, or his rent-roll, that gave Lord Salisbury his power over his countrymen and Europe. Lord Salisbury won his place by much the same virtues as other men have used to raise themselves from humble positions. He was an indefatigable worker, sitting at his desk, it is said, for thirteen out of the twenty-four hours. He certainly answered, with his own hand, and at considerable length, correspondents who wrote to him on subjects which he thought interesting or important, quite regardless of the rank of the writer, a species of courtesy which other smaller men might profitably imitate. As a specimen of his real modesty and fine courtesy to a young and unofficial supporter, who had asked his assistance, I subjoin an autograph letter :—

Private

Dec. 15. 92.

Dear Mr. Baumann

I am very glad to hear that you are going to write on betterment. It requires such an investigation as I am sure you will give to it — its true place in reference to the general principles of taxation ought to be ascertained — & I am convinced that the result, to any dispassionate & scientific enquirer will be such as I foresee.

Under ordinary circumstances I should be very glad to associate myself with you in this undertaking — if you thought that such coöperation as you indicate was likely to be useful. But the expediency of my doing so is a good deal affected by the fact that I am — though on a humble scale — a London land-owner myself. This of course will not prevent me from fighting in the ranks with other Parliamentary friends, if the occasion should arise. But it makes me doubt the wisdom of my coming forward by your side as a champion upon the question. I am afraid that the enemy instead of answering

your arguments, will confine themselves to sarcasms on my interested motives.

This, & this alone, makes me think that I ought not to act on your suggestion.

Yours very truly
Salisbury

Private.

Dear Mr. Baumann,

I am very glad to hear that you are going to write on " betterment." It requires such an investigation as I am sure you will give to it—its true place in reference to the general principles of taxation ought to be ascertained : and I am convinced that the result, to any dispassionate and scientific enquirer will be such as you foresee.

Under ordinary circumstances I should be very glad to associate myself with you in this undertaking—if you thought that such co-operation as you indicate was likely to be useful. But the expediency of my doing so is a good deal affected by the fact that I am—though on a humble scale—a London landowner myself. This of course will not prevent me from fighting in the ranks with other Parliamentary friends, if the occasion should arise. But it makes me doubt the wisdom of my coming forward by your side as a champion upon the question. I am afraid that the enemy instead of answering your arguments, will confine themselves to sarcasms on my interested motives.

This, and this alone, makes me think that I ought not to act on your suggestion.

Yours very truly,
Salisbury.

There was only one kind of intellectual drudgery which he refused, that, namely, of writing out his speeches before delivery.

Whether he was constitutionally incapable of remembering a manuscript, or whether he thought that the result was not worth the labour, I do not know. But the habit of not writing even notes beforehand prevented Lord Salisbury's speeches from ranking as oratory. For though the style was incisive and correct, generally humorous and sometimes witty, it was too disjointed and familiar to be read in print by posterity. Indeed, Lord Salisbury despised rhetoric, just as he despised self-advertisement, and sham philanthropy, and the other demagogic arts. Sometimes his simplicity was very dramatic. Addressing a huge meeting of working men in a South London music-hall, the Prime Minister wiped his brow with the back of his hand. The familiar gesture at once put an audience of shy artisans at their ease. He dealt with the Balkan question. "I have in my pocket," said Lord Salisbury, "a letter from the Sultan of Turkey, which I will read to you," and, fumbling in the breast-pocket of his frock-coat, he pulled out a bundle of letters, from which he selected one, and said, "The Sultan asks me to tell the People of England," and then began to read a few words about Turkish reform probably dictated by the British Ambassador at Constantinople. The artisans, clerks, and dock labourers gasped with excitement. Here was a man who walked about with letters from the crowned heads of Europe jumbled up with his ordinary correspondence! And this man was standing there talking to them! This was something like politics!

At other times his simplicity had the effect of an Olympian rebuke. During one of the violent phases of the Irish question between '85 and '92 some credulous Radical wrote to Lord Salisbury asking whether it was true, as reported in the papers, that he had signed a treaty with Mr. Parnell in the smoking-room of the House of Commons, to which the following reply was sent :—" Sir,—Lord Salisbury desires me to say, (1) he has never seen Mr. Parnell; (2) he has never been in the smoking-room of the House of Commons. I am, Sir, yours faithfully," etc.

This contempt for popularity was, of course, one of the sources of his power over the democracy. It must, however, be admitted that in what may be called the lyrical power of statesmen, the power of saying in great language what the nation is thinking, Lord Salisbury was exasperatingly deficient. It was not that he failed "to read their history in a nation's eyes"; no man saw further or more clearly ahead than Lord Salisbury; but he scorned to avail himself of what Burke called " swelling sentiments " for the purpose of encouragement or consolation. At the beginning of the Boer War, for instance, when everybody was in despair at our reverses, and when the nation was thirsting for a patriotic speech, the Prime Minister stolidly declined to be dithyrambic, and persisted in treating Colenso as a twopenny-halfpenny Somaliland affair. It is very likely that this apparent apathy and levity concealed a deep policy with regard to foreign nations; but at the time it was chilling and disappointing. Partly, I think, it was due to his health, which ebbed with the century. I heard him make one of his last speeches in the House of Lords, in which he warned the nation against overtaxing its strength by a policy of military adventure. But the drowsiness of delivery made me sad, as I knew the end could not be far off.

The austerity of Lord Salisbury's habits was another factor which contributed to his influence. Nothing impresses the masses more than the spectacle of a man, who might gratify all the senses of the voluptuary, living simply, and devoting himself to the public service. He never smoked, for even the fumes of a cigarette gave him a headache. He ate heartily, like all men who use their brains hard, but to the pleasures of the table, in the epicurean sense, he was a stranger. He was conspicuously careless in his dress, and he was not interested in his horses and carriages. In his old age he was seen riding a tricycle down to the Foreign Office with flying coat tails and a soft black hat. He neither hunted nor shot, though on rare occasions he carried a gun about the park at Hatfield in company with his boys. When people said that Lord Salisbury was a cynic they meant that he did not believe in legislation as a cure for social ills. They could not mean it in any other sense. For he was a religious man, attached to the Church, and with strong family affections, as I have already observed. Though his pride and shyness prevented him from mixing easily with his fellows, and though most of his supporters in the House of Commons and some of his colleagues outside the Cabinet were unknown to him by sight, his nature was so generous that he was sometimes imposed upon by importunity and impudence.

Once you had gained access to him, Lord Salisbury's courtesy was exquisite, and he assumed the soothing manner of a family physician. In legislation he assuredly did not believe, and it is not therefore as a law-maker that he will fill his niche in history. The Bill for the creation of Parish Councils had been advocated on the ground that it would amuse the rural population. "I deny," said Lord Salisbury, "that it is the duty of Government to provide amusement for the people. But if that be any part of its function, I should suggest a circus."

Lord Salisbury's reputation will rest on the following achievements. He defeated, and actually killed, the Home Rule that would have subjected North East Ulster to the government of Celtic South and West Ireland; he kept the peace between Britain and the United States when President Cleveland sent his insulting message respecting Venezuela, and between Britain and France when Colonel Marchand was minded to hoist the tricolour at Fashoda; he stopped the European Powers from helping Spain in its quarrel with the United States over Cuba; and he prevented the intervention of the European powers in our South African War. The two latter diplomatic victories he won by clearly explaining that whoever fought against the Americans or with the Boers would have to fight England. And Europe shut up like a telescope at the sight of Lord Salisbury's teeth.

In each of these great triumphs of statesmanship may be detected the ground-note of his character and career. Lord Salisbury was not an orator; nor a party manager; nor a propounder of programmes. But he was one of the greatest Prime Ministers of the last century, because he had the power of sobriety, the quality which the Greeks called σωφροσύνη, the sane and fearless mind, working without friction in its proper plane.

Sir William Harcourt

SIR WILLIAM HARCOURT

THE combination of the lawyer and the politician is more often successful than any other in our public life. In a popular assembly, which governs by discussion, the lawyer's tongue will, as a rule, carry a man further than weight of purse or length of pedigree. They may say what they like about lawyers being unpopular and despised in the House of Commons. It is untrue. Lawyers can find words when other men are dumb; and the success of Brougham, Clarke, Carson, Asquith, Haldane, and F. E. Smith refutes the popular dictum. Mr. Vernon Harcourt appeared at the parliamentary bar just before the great tide of railway business that made the fortunes of Charles Austin and Hope Scott had ebbed. In 1855 a young man belonging to an aristocratic Yorkshire family, with a fine voice and a tall figure, had still an opening. Mr. Vernon Harcourt took full advantage of his opportunity. It was at this time that the antagonism between Sir Edmund Beckett, the first Lord Grimthorpe, and the future Minister developed itself. Nearly thirty years later, when Beckett was leader of the parliamentary bar and Harcourt was Home Secretary, it burst again into flame during the inquiry by a committee into the purchase of the London water companies. In the ten or twelve years that he practised, it is said that Vernon Harcourt made between £30,000 and £40,000, and with this sum he ventured his barque upon the ocean of politics. Although Vernon Harcourt entered Parliament as a lawyer, and although in 1873 Gladstone made him Solicitor-General, in the technical or tradesman sense of the term he never was a lawyer. It is hardly necessary to say that practice at the parliamentary bar has nothing to do with law. The proceedings before committees on private bills are inquiries into facts by a lay tribunal, which does not even observe the law of evidence, though it reluctantly listens to gentlemen of the robe. Vernon Harcourt, it is true, made a reputation by writing letters to the *Times* on International Law, which were full of erudition and acumen. But International Law, again, is an historical subject, and has nothing to do with the law of the Courts of Justice. If we except Sir John Gorst, there probably never was a Solicitor-General who knew less about his business than Sir William Harcourt, as no one knew better than himself. From 1874 to 1880 Sir William Harcourt passed through that most uncomfortable period, which comes to all politicians, when they are not sure whether they are going to sink into hell or rise to heaven. Sir William Harcourt had practically abandoned his profession; he had fallen foul of Gladstone over Church matters; and he was being encouraged by Disraeli. The election of 1880 changed all that. Gladstone's Midlothian speeches rather overshadowed the other participants in the fray. But next to the Chief, Sir William Harcourt undoubtedly stood out as a great electioneering gladiator. He was rewarded by being made Home Secretary, and in 1880 Sir William Harcourt passed with a bound from the rank of a political adventurer to that of a statesman of the first class.

A great Minister of State, a powerful leader of Opposition, Sir William Harcourt was; but he was much more—a great personality. Apart from one or two on each side, how few ministers have any individuality of their own! The late Mr. Childers, for instance, filled all the highest offices of State except that of First Lord of the Treasury; yet what impression did his character make upon the House of Commons, or the Civil Service, or society? Absolutely none. Strip Mr. Ritchie of his portfolio, and what remained? A very commonplace Member of Parliament, whom no one would mark in public or private life. Now Sir William Harcourt, whether he was on the Front Bench or in Downing Street, at a dinner-table or on the platform, or in his own library, was always a great individuality. The effect he produced was of course much helped by his presence and his name. Had he been a dunce and a plebeian, you could not have overlooked him in a room. Being a wit, a scholar, and Vernon Harcourt, he was irresistible. I remember, very many years ago, that Sir William Harcourt was last on the toast list at the opening of the Palmerston Club at Oxford. It was near midnight when he rose, and he had the tact to throw over his written speech, and to indulge in a quarter of an hour's most exquisite chaff and pointed conversation.

All Harcourt's fun and tenderness and hard wit are poured into his letters, which are better than Walpole's or Gray's, and as good as Byron's and Disraeli's. Here is a sample of playfulness. In the winter of 1886, with the wounds of the great split still smarting, Harcourt writes to invite Chamberlain and Jesse Collings, who had just returned from a tour in Turkey, to stay with him at Malwood, " I am glad to see that you have returned from your ticket of leave. The late Home Secretary " (himself) " will wink hard at this breach of prison regulations. You have probably returned from the East in a state of deplorable ignorance as to the state of civilization in the West, especially in the Westernmost of the British islands. As I am always desirous to enlighten the benighted, I feel a yearning to see you. In the New Forest a fez and loose breeches will not attract attention. Pray come and see us. If you are accompanied by the father of the dissolute David (Jesse Collings), the chief eunuch of your seraglio, we shall be all the better pleased. He will find here plenty of Uriahs with an allotment and a ewe lamb apiece, though I fear he has abandoned all these early enthusiasms of his agrarian innocence." Who can, or cares to, write such letters now ?

In society Harcourt was never at a loss for a retort. His comment on Randolph Churchill's proposed Centre Party that it would be " all centre and no circumference " is Sheridanesque ; and when Hartington expressed surprise at meeting him under the roof of Lord Londonderry, " the author of the Union," he was smashed by the answer: "Remember that the author of the Union ended by cutting his throat, and you had better take that as a warning." As a public speaker, Harcourt was at his best on the platform. His huge figure dominated the biggest meeting, and, without vulgarity or malice, he thwacked his opponents resonantly with anecdotes, sarcasm, humorous illustration, fairly romping into the hearts of his audience. In the House of Commons he was at his worst, posing as the heavy statesman. I sat opposite him for seven years ('85 to '92), and I loved him all the time, because he was an anti-humbug man, and because he sweetened debate by his unfailing urbanity. But I am bound to say that his long speeches were often very tiresome. His voice was unmusical and without variety, and he would read page after page of notes. His flashes of fun were few and far between—a ha'porth of bread to an intolerable amount of sack.

Of course, Harcourt was neither Whig nor Tory, nor Radical, but all three. Men of first-rate mental calibre who go into politics—"business," as they called it in the eighteenth century—belong to no party but to all parties. It was so with Burke, it was so with Disraeli. Even the sanctimonious Gladstone passed the first quarter of his life as a Tory, the second quarter as a Peelite, the third quarter as a Liberal, and the fourth quarter as a Home-Ruler. It is chance more often than choice that decides the flag under which these very clever men are to march. Harcourt happened to get elected at Oxford in 1868 as a Liberal; but he would have served Disraeli even more effectively than he did Gladstone, and it was an accident that he did not do so.

After a few months as Solicitor-General in 1873-4, and the interval of Lord Beaconsfield's Government, Harcourt became in 1880 Home Secretary. It was unfortunate for him that the following five years were the most terrible in the history of Irish Nationalism. There were the Phœnix Park murders, the Kilmainham Treaty, O'Donovan Rossa and the dynamite explosions; while all the time Harcourt was learning from Scotland Yard the horrible secrets of Parnell's private life, which were not confined to Eltham. The Home Secretary was a Cromwellian at heart, and knew, as all sensible men know, that murder and arson and robbery can only be put down by hanging and imprisonment. With crimes labelled political he had not the smallest sentimental sympathy, and accordingly he put the law into force with rapidity and vigour. When the great split came, and Harcourt followed Gladstone, the fury of the Tories was concentrated on Harcourt, whom they abused ten times more bitterly than his chief. How was it possible, they asked, that a man who had almost danced on the bodies of his prisoners, who had left the Tories to " stew in their Parnellite juice," who kept up his private friendship with Hartington and Chamberlain, who was a born territorial aristocrat—how could a man who did and was all these things be a sincere Home Ruler? Harcourt's explanation, given unfortunately not in public, but in his letters and conversations, was that when he saw in 1885 the Tories agreeing not to renew the Crimes Act, Carnarvon meeting Parnell in an empty house, Churchill and Beach promising an enquiry into the Maamtrasna murders, he recognized that intermittent coercion was no longer possible as a means of governing Ireland. It was a perfectly sound defence. But why did not Harcourt make his explanation in public? If he had done so, much would have been forgiven him, including his irrepressible jokes, and his habit of dining with his political opponents.

In 1892, the constituencies " gave the G.O.M. a last chance," and Harcourt became Chancellor of the Exchequer. He passed the most famous Budget of modern times, establishing the death duties. The basic principle of these duties is false and vicious, as it takes the accumulated savings, or capital, of the nation and spends it as annual revenue; and it was a curious Nemesis that Nuneham was one of the first estates to suffer by its owner's financial blunder. Then followed the tragedy of 1894. After Gladstone had tendered his resignation to the Queen, she did not ask his advice as to whom she should send for, a strange lapse of propriety, and of constitutional precedent. Had she done so, we know that Gladstone would have advised her sending for Lord Spencer. The timid and prejudiced old woman, with one foot in the grave, ignored Harcourt, and threw her handkerchief to a debonnair young noble. It reminds me of Queen Anne on her deathbed, gazing with frightened eyes at Bolingbroke, and feebly pushing the White Staff into the hands of Shrewsbury. I cannot blame the old Queen, but I do blame the meanness and snobbishness of the Liberal leaders, who humbly submitted to the Royal mandate; above all, I cannot excuse the treachery of Morley, who, if he had stood by Harcourt, would have rendered impossible the formation of a Government by Rosebery.

In the lives of all men of action, especially on the political stage, there are passages which their friends would be glad to cover up, since they cannot be satisfactorily explained. My respect and admiration for Lord Morley have been recently increased by reading his "Recollections," Mr. J. H. Morgan's monograph, and Sir Almeric Fitzroy's account of his intercourse with his Lord President of the Council. I wish I could find an honourable explanation of Morley's desertion of Harcourt, whom he had promised to support as Gladstone's successor two years previously, before Rosebery was thought of. It is certain that in 1894 Morley, who was sick of his job as Irish Secretary, coveted the seals of the Foreign Office. If Harcourt became Prime Minister Rosebery would retain the Foreign Secretaryship. But if Rosebery became Prime Minister, he would probably vacate the Foreign Office, which Morley would then claim, and I have been told that there was no office in the Cabinets of 1895 and 1905, including the Premier's, to which Morley did not at one time or another advance the claim of seniority. If that was Morley's calculation, his abandonment of Harcourt was unrewarded, for Rosebery appointed Kimberley to the Foreign Office. But Morley may honestly have thought with Asquith that Harcourt was almost impossible as a colleague, and quite impossible as a leader. In truth Harcourt was too fond of dismissing all opinions that crossed his own as " damned nonsense." He called himself an eighteenth century man like Hartington, and gloried in the name of Philistine.

This is how Morley put it to Harcourt, who, with a conventional insincerity quite unusual to him, had declared that he didn't want to be leader. " My dear Harcourt, forgive me for being frank. But you deceive yourself. You do want to be leader. You are a proud man. You are aristocratic to your finger tips. People may say *stemmata quid faciunt?* if they like, but your *stemma* interests you immensely. What is the use of genealogies ? Quite right, too. You have had a Chancellor in your family, and a Lord Lietutenant of Ireland, and you'd like to have a Prime Minister in your family, and no earthly blame to you. The thing for us and for the Party has a double aspect, how we can best carry on the fight in the House of Commons between now and the dissolution, and how we can offer the best front when the election comes. From the first point of view you are nothing less than indispensable ; from the second the advantages are with Rosebery." These last words were expanded to show Harcourt how far more interesting to the public than himself was a rich fashionable peer who owned a probable Derby winner. Harcourt cannot have relished these explanations, and a few years later he accosted Morley with the remark, " So you're going to write Mr. G's life ? An excellent choice ! There's no man better qualified than you, except, of course, on the religious question—you must not touch that ; or his financial policy—you don't understand finance ; or Home Rule—you've got a bee in your bonnet about that." These encounters of wit leave stings behind them ; and on the whole Harcourt seems to have felt more at home with his old friends of the Bar. To Lord James he wrote, " there's nothing like old wine and old friends : you are my choicest bin." Driving home from a political meeting at Hackney with Sir Charles Russell, then Attorney-General, Harcourt asked his opinion as a friend whether he, Harcourt, had enough law for the Woolsack. Russell answered " if you had asked me for a county court judge, I should have said No. But for the Lord Chancellor, oh yes." Harcourt would have enjoyed that joke, which is quite in the style of the Bar.

There is no doubt that Harcourt's breeziness and chaff offended a good many people. Gazing down from his massive height upon Lord Charles Beresford's dapper figure, in tight frock coat and glossy curly brimmed topper, he said appraisingly, " You know, Charlie, you don't look like a statesman." Charlie was visibly annoyed, for in the House of Commons he took himself seriously. He answered, not inaptly, "You know, Harcourt, you don't look like a weathercock." Across the floor of the House frequently Harcourt could be heard in a stage whisper commanding one of his minor colleagues not to make a damned fool of himself.

A word or two about the Jameson Raid. There is no doubt that Harcourt ultimately believed that Chamberlain was implicated, if not in the Raid itself, certainly in the preparations for that crime. I agree with Mr. Gardiner in his Life of Sir William Harcourt* that the cutting short the inquiry at the precise point where Chamberlain's complicity was at issue was ambiguous and unsatisfactory. His only motives could have been his friendship for Chamberlain and his desire to avoid a scandal : they are not enough. Harcourt, in his correspondence, after the Committee on the Raid, always referred to Rhodes as "the arch-liar." It certainly was remarkable that the Report condemning Rhodes in the strongest terms for having violated his privy councillor's oath by deceiving the High Commissioner, for having planned and financed the invasion of a friendly State as Prime Minister of the Cape Colony, should have been " laid " on the table of the House of Commons without a word from Sir William Harcourt, and without the Committee's " asking for leave to sit again." Vain attempts were subsequently made to discuss the report, which only elicited from Chamberlain the declaration that Rhodes had done nothing "to affect his personal position as

**Life of Sir William Harcourt*, by A. G. Gardiner. 2 Vols. Constable.

a man of honour." I believe that a future generation will read with amazement the immunity accorded to Rhodes, while Dr. Jameson and the officers who rode with him were indicted for a breach of the Foreign Enlistment Act, and cast into prison. That Rhodes did not stand with them in the dock is a grave reflection on the Unionist Government.

Mr. Gardiner has taken infinite pains to get into the skin of his subject and he has so succeeded that great will be his reward. The " Conclusion " is the justest, and the most penetrating appreciation of a public man's character and career that I have read. The performance is the more creditable because the dissector is an Idealist, and the dissected was a Realist, a Philistine as he loved to call himself, of the earth earthy. It is true that Sir William Harcourt missed the two prizes, which in the alternative he set out to win, the Woolsack and the Premiership. But he would not have increased his reputation had he gained either; probably the reverse. He could not have been a great Lord Chancellor; he had not enough Law. In the year that was left to him before the election, with a divided party behind him, he could not have been a successful Prime Minister. By students of political finance, he will be remembered as the author of the death duties, which he was one of the first to pay. The larger class who read their country's history in the lives of its first men will think of him as a splendid gladiator, a loyal partisan, a staunch friend, and a great English gentleman, with the generosity and the recklessness of his order.

Viscount Goschen

VISCOUNT GOSCHEN

To those who study the art of success in this world — as who does not? — the beginning of a great man's career is always more interesting than the end. As soon as the biography of a great personage appears, it is seized on by old and young, who say, " Here was a successful man ! Now let me try to find out the secret of his success, so that I may see how I too can succeed, or why I have failed." Alas, for the ambitious and the disappointed ! The successful man cannot communicate his secret, for the simple reason that he does not know it. I have tried the experiment on several millionaires of my acquaintance, asking each of them how he made his fortune. Not one of them could tell me ; though all uttered vigorous platitudes about industry and perseverance. As if there were not a million men who trudge past the Bank on three hundred days in the year, all full of industry and perseverance ! A late friend of mine, once high in the Councils of the Unionist party, told me that when he was staying at Seacox Heath, just after Goschen had become Chancellor of the Exchequer, his host asked him, with great earnestness, " I want you to tell me this : Why do you young Tories believe in me ?" " We believe in you, Mr. Goschen," was the answer, " because we believe that you stand for principle in public life."

And this was the secret of his success, although, of course, he did not know it.

It is impossible not to be struck by the ease and rapidity with which Goschen was hoisted to the top of the political ladder—so different from the terrible early struggles of Disraeli. Better it would have been for Goschen had his path not been quite so smooth, for though the temple of fame should never be inaccessible to genius, it should stand upon a hill, not to be climbed without difficulty and danger. Both young men started under the heavy handicap of a foreign name; but from the fact that this never seemed to hinder Goschen in any way, one is driven to the conclusion that a great deal of the abuse and prejudice which Disraeli encountered was his own fault. Every man's hand was against Disraeli, because Disraeli's hand was against every man: one who gives no quarter receives none. Goschen never dealt in personal invective, which was Disraeli's daily bread. Then again, the foreign angles were rubbed off young Goschen at Rugby and Oriel; while Disraeli was left to educate himself in his father's library, or in a seminary for young gentlemen. Further, Goschen's father was a wealthy and well-known foreign banker in the City; and freedom from pecuniary cares—an enormous advantage in politics—attended Goschen from his cradle to his grave. After leaving Oriel, where he took a first in Greats, Goschen passed ten years in his father's firm, whose business was that of accepting bills of exchange. An Oxford first-class man does not spend a decade in handling bills of foreign exchange without getting to understand, not only the practice, but the principles underlying the business. This accident enabled Goschen to write a clear-headed book on a subject which is Chinese to men outside the City, and is only dimly comprehended in Lombard Street. There was probably only one man in the last century, besides Goschen, who could have written *The Theory of Foreign Exchange*; I mean Walter Bagehot. The leading bankers in the City, the Rothschilds and the Barings and the Curries, were not slow to perceive that here was a young man, who combined the culture of Oxford with a knowledge of their own mysteries greater than that possessed by themselves. At twenty-seven Goschen was chosen a director of the Bank of England; and at thirty-two he was elected, at a bye-election in 1863, one of the Members for the City. His reputation preceded him to Westminster. He was clutched from Austin Friars by Lord Russell, as Disraeli describes Pitt clutching his banker-peers from Change Alley, for then, as now, a Member of Parliament, who had any real acquaintance with finance, was a rare bird. After the general election and Lord Palmerston's death in 1865, Lord Russell formed a Government in which he included Goschen as Vice-President of the Board of Trade, and a few months later this favourite of fortune entered the Cabinet as Chancellor of the Duchy. He had then been only two years and a half in the House of Commons, and was only thirty-four years old! The thing is prodigious, and without a precedent, so far as I know, in the political history of the nineteenth century. When Gladstone formed his Cabinet in 1868, Goschen became First Lord of the Admiralty, a post for which he was well suited, for his industry, his capacity of learning details, his power of organisation, and his ardent patriotism, were just what are wanted in the head of the Navy. Goschen did not take a seat in Gladstone's Government in 1880, though, of course, invited, for a reason which revealed his greatness of character. The extension of the residential borough franchise to the counties had already been mooted by the Radicals, and Goschen had spoken and voted against it, an honest and courageous act in a Liberal statesman.

Instead of entering the Cabinet, Goschen accepted a special diplomatic mission to Constantinople, which, together with the affairs of Egypt, occupied a great deal of his time. It was in 1884 and 1885, after the borough franchise had been extended to the counties, that the rift in the Liberal party began first to appear. Mr. Joseph Chamberlain delivered in these years a series of speeches against the rich and the House of Lords. Goschen was angry and disgusted, as we see from his correspondence, and set to work, together with Lord Hartington, to counteract this Socialistic propaganda. Gladstone was at that time pondering whether he should throw in his lot with Goschen and Hartington, with Chamberlain and Dilke, or with Parnell.

We know Gladstone's decision and its consequences. Mr. Arthur Elliot's Life of Lord Goschen give one a vivid insight into the feelings, first of incredulity, then of rage and alarm, with which the moderate Liberals learned Gladstone's intention to hand Ireland over to the man whom he had imprisoned and denounced as "marching through rapine to the dismemberment of the Empire." However, in a few weeks they had to choose between Gladstone's Bill and "giving a blank cheque" to Lord Salisbury. Goschen never really hesitated for more than a few days. Gladstone's ambiguities and the lies of the party hacks and the Press angered him, for Goschen could not be obscure if he tried, and he was the soul of political honesty. Lord Randolph Churchill flung himself out of office in a rage six months after the formation of the Salisbury Government, and the Chancellorship of the Exchequer was accepted by Goschen. Paradoxical as it may seem, it was the post for which he was least fitted, and in which he was least successful. He had six surpluses to dispose of, yet he did nothing with them by which he will live in the minds of men. He declared that the basis of taxation was too narrow; but he did nothing to widen it. His "wheel and van" and "pleasure horse" taxes covered him with ridicule, and had to be dropped. He converted Consols from 3's to $2\frac{3}{4}$, and finally to $2\frac{1}{2}$ per cents.; and it is true that this conversion in 1888 saved the nation a quarter per cent. for twelve years—some twenty millions or so. But twelve years are a drop in the ocean of a nation's life; and the only real justification for such a step is the maintenance of the national security at or about par. If $2\frac{3}{4}$ per cent. Consols fall to a 3 per cent. basis (which is what happened) there is only a temporary saving to the nation; but there is the annoyance of seeing the national funds at a discount, and the loss to those who have bought. By July, 1901, after the South African war loans had begun, Consols fell to 91, and in April, 1903, they fell to $89\frac{7}{8}$. So that when the nation came to borrow for war in 1901 it had to pay 3 per cent. after all.

Of course Goschen could not have foreseen the South African War, nor Mr. Chamberlain's Colonial Stock Act of 1900. But it is surely nothing more than common prudence to assume that there will be war some time or other. Nor is it the mark of a great Chancellor of the Exchequer to base your calculations on the continuance of a bank-rate at 2 per cent. and of Consols at 107. It was the cheapness of money in the market, due to the stagnation of trade, that misled Goschen. But he ought, with his experience, to have known that it was an abnormal, and therefore a temporary cheapness. I remember Harcourt saying to Goschen in the House, in savagely exultant tones, " Consols will fall as surely as the barometer." Besides, the reduction of interest always inflicts loss of income upon a considerable and generally helpless class—hardly the policy of a Conservative Chancellor. Lord Randolph Churchill had no pretensions to being a professional financier, but he had a double dose of mother-wit, and he wrote to Goschen the following sagacious criticisms on his conversion scheme : " It is not and cannot be popular, except with those who do not hold Consols. I suppose an immense proportion of fund-holders have purchased their stock at 100, or even under, and 3 per cents. at $102\frac{1}{2}$, to the popular instinct, which does not count as closely as might be thought, a more desirable and attractive possession than $2\frac{1}{2}$ per cents at 96 or 95. Nor do I think you can afford to pay off at such a price and on such terms as will satisfy those who have purchased at par, or under, that they have not been done out of a legitimate gain, and those who have purchased above par that they have not been forced into a loss. Besides which there are all the old women and old men in the country who like to get 3 per cent. and do not like to get $2\frac{1}{8}$ per cent." (*Life of Lord Goschen*, vol. ii, p. 148). Assuredly Randolph Churchill could not have written *The Theory of the Foreign Exchanges*, his knowledge of bills being probably confined to " bits of blue " discounted in Jermyn Street, and he did not understand " those damned dots " in the Treasury sums ; but he would have made a better Chancellor of the Exchequer than Goschen. Another instance of Goschen's want of knowledge of human nature was his joint attempt with Ritchie—the evil genius of the Tory party—to provide a fund for buying up licences by putting extra taxes on beer and spirits. Goschen was innocent enough to believe that the moderate men in the temperance party, and the moderate men in the liquor trade would unite to support this proposal. As if the moderate men in any party ever united to support anybody or anything! Of course Sir Wilfrid Lawson convened a monster demonstration to protest against buying up licences, and of course the publicans counter-demonstrated against extra taxation. The extra taxes were put on all the same, but the licences were not bought up, the money being devoted to technical education! This did not enhance Goschen's popularity, and damaged the Government. The truth was that Goschen's City training in a bill-acceptor's office, so useful to him in other ways, militated against his success at the Treasury. Goschen took broad and spirited views on everything except money. When money was in question, the old habit of dealing in fractions was strong upon him, and he became meticulous.

Knowledge of the world, not close calculation, is what makes a good Chancellor of the Exchequer. Sir William Harcourt and Sir Michael Hicks-Beach were the two best Chancellors of the Exchequer in the late Victorian period, and the first was a lawyer, and the second was a country gentleman. It is astonishing how few, even among clever and well-informed people realise that finance in Downing Street is a very different thing from finance in Lombard Street.

Confounding the two, the most powerful and famous of American financiers made a mistake. He wanted a man to manage his London business, and he applied to the Treasury (of all places) for a financier. The

Treasury gave him one of their best financiers, one of Goschen's private secretaries, who had been brilliantly successful as Finance Minister in Egypt and in India. The result was hardly a success. The Treasury financier did not understand the language of the brokers in the City, and was slow to catch their point of view. It would have been strange had it been otherwise. The political financier must take long, broad, sympathetic views; the City financier must take short, narrow, unsympathetic views. The financial statesman must trust much to the better instincts of mankind: the commercial magnate must trust to them not at all.

Goschen had something very like a panic to deal with during his reign at the Treasury, and he showed great firmness and prudence. The great house of Baring had succumbed to the temptations of an American speculator, and had " bitten off more than it could chew " in the matter of Argentine securities. A smash was imminent in 1890, and the Governor and directors of the Bank of England pressed the Chancellor of the Exchequer very hard to come to the rescue by joining in a guarantee fund to tide the Barings over the crisis. It must have been hard for Goschen to refuse, for the Barings were old friends. and he must have perfectly appreciated their difficulty, But that was where Goschen's greatness always came in. When he saw the right course, he allowed no consideration on earth to prevent him from pursuing it. He saw clearly that it would be wrong for the Government to assist a private individual with public money, and he at once decided not to do so. Let the Bank of England and the other banks subscribe to get the Barings out, he said; and this was done, as a guarantee fund of some £18,000,000 was put up, and averted a smash. This suggests food for reflection for the cynic. If you smash for £10,000 you are a fool; if you smash for £100,000 you are a rogue; but if you smash for £10,000,000, you are a martyr, and must be tenderly nursed by the Old Lady of Threadneedle Street. Goschen, however, would have nothing to do with the nursing.

On the whole, looking back on the six years that Goschen was Chancellor of the Exchequer, I am not surprised that Lord Salisbury reverted in 1895 to "Black Michael," and replaced Goschen at the Admiralty, where he was in his element, and one of the very best First Lords the Navy ever obeyed. He was full of enthusiasm for the Service, and no one appreciated more clearly the necessity of keeping up the two-power standard. Luckily for Goschen's reputation and happiness, he was out of the miserable business of 1903 with its intrigues and resignations—the beginning of the end. He had retired in 1900 from the House of Commons and had been made a Viscount.

Goschen was a Free Trader; indeed, it was impossible that he should be anything else, unless he changed his opinions, and he was not the man to change opinions which he had held up to the age of seventy-two because Mr. Chamberlain or anybody else had changed. If he would not change his Irish policy for Gladstone, he was not likely to change his fiscal policy for Chamberlain. Colonial preference he denounced as gambling with the people's food; and from the serene heights of the House of Lords he kept firing big guns at the Tariff Reform position. Whether we agree or disagree with Lord Goschen's fiscal policy, we must admire the lucidity and vigour of his last speeches and pamphlets on this question. Courage, truthfulness, enthusiasm, and unselfishness are great moral qualities; and when they are combined with extraordinary intellectual energy and the rhetorical gift, their possessor must become, in this country, a great statesman. The intellectual gifts remain with our politicians; but the moral qualities, which won for Goschen the admiration of friend and foe, are fast disappearing from our public life.

Goschen had a nice sense of language, but solely as the vehicle of argument or denunciation. His English was crisp, clear, and mordacious; but of oratory as an art he was contemptuous. Very early in his career (1868) an old friend, Mr. Cracroft, wrote to him as follows: "You must make style as style, and elocution as elocution, your study for some hours a day for the next few years. You know what practising means, for you play the piano, and you must practise the very scales and rudiments of elocution . . . In your speech as reported in the *Star* evidently verbatim, I find three consecutive sentences out of four beginning with 'Now,' showing that you were quite at a loss to cover your sequence. Now sequence is one of the first elements—mechanical, but essential elements—of anything that can be called oratory." His friend tells Goschen that he is in the third rank of orators, instead of in the first rank with Lowe, and Bright, and Gladstone, " and all because pride and prejudice will not allow you to study what is an art, but which you choose to consider artifice. On your part this seems to me a most distressing piece of littleness of mind." And then Mr. Cracroft goes on to point out the advantage of acquiring " a repose and command of manner . . . the power of evolution—the habit of beginning quietly, and expanding comfortably, and with measured convenience to your audience what you want to say. The study of a measured delivery would help to strengthen the throat. Nothing affects the throat more fundamentally than unrhythmical agitation." (*Life of Lord Goschen*, vol. 1, p. 104). It was perhaps too much to expect a Cabinet Minister to spend some hours every day practising the rudiments of elocution, as it was said Murray and Wedderburn did, before a looking glass, in their early years. But it was a pity that Goschen did not take at least some of his friend's advice, for the physical defects of his oratory greatly marred its effect. Goschen, however, had a greater capacity for not taking advice than anybody; he listened and continued his own course. He had no repose; he was always in a state of " unrhythmical agitation," which did seem to affect his throat, for his voice was raucous and husky. His style was jagged and disjointed; there were no *callidæ juncturæ* to piece together the members of the argument. His speeches were a torrent or a tempest, and I always wondered how they were followed by the reporters. He threw his head backwards and forwards, and from side to side; he peered through the bars of an imaginary ghetto; and he had a trick of flinging out his right arm as if he would seize his antagonist by the throat. He was so excitable that no one was more easily " derailed " by an interjection; and to " draw Goschen " became a favourite pastime with the Irish.

Mr. Healy once said with his most sibilant sneer, " The right hon. gentleman has been descanting on the Christian virtues, a subject on which he is, of course, so well qualified to speak." Goschen rose from the Treasury bench pale and furious. " And why am I not qualified to speak on the Christian virtues ?" W. H. Smith pulled Goschen down on to the bench by his coat-tails, saying soothingly, " Never mind him; take no notice."

The allusion was, of course, to the prevalent idea that Goschen was of Jewish origin. The publication of his grandfather's life by Lord Goschen, and Mr. Arthur Elliot's biography, correct this mistake as far as religion is concerned, as they show that the family had been Lutheran for at least three generations. But if he was not a Jew by race, nature has forgotten how to use her antique pen. Goschen was always very sensitive to personal attacks, and he never failed to display extraordinary irritation when Mr. Labouchere teased him about Messrs. Frühling and Göschen's interest in Egyptian bonds.

On another occasion he swept his arm jeeringly towards the Irish benches. " Ah, yes ; I marked those Irish cheers, that Celtic music, which is always so sweet to the ears of the right hon. gentleman " (Gladstone). " It's sweeter than the Jew's harp, anyway," shouted an Irishman. It was painful to witness the rage which almost choked his further utterance.

Of those great qualities, earnestness and enthusiasm, the defects are restlessness and excitability. It is to be regretted that Goschen did not cultivate the graces of manner and style. Chesterfield went so far as to say that the matter of all speeches was common property and that it was the manner and the words that made an orator's success.

Of a greater man than Goschen it was said by Moore : " In vain did Burke's genius put forth its superb plumage, glittering all over with the hundred eyes of fancy—the gait of the bird was heavy and awkward, and its voice seemed rather to scare than to attract." Goschen was no dealer in epigrams, but occasionally his phrases stuck. " I will not give Lord Salisbury a blank cheque," and, " Let us make our wills and do our duty," are perhaps his two most famous sayings.

Not the least interesting passage in Mr. Elliot's book is the interchange of letters between Lord Salisbury,

Mr. Balfour, and Goschen about the leadership of the House of Commons, vacant in consequence of the death of W. H. Smith in 1891. Sir Michael Hicks Beach was at this time suffering from his eyesight, and the choice therefore lay between Mr. Balfour and Goschen. Lord Salisbury wrote: " You possess, in our judgment, all the qualities required for a House of Commons leader at this juncture, *except one*; that you are not a member of the political party which furnishes much the largest portion of the Unionist phalanx." Lord Salisbury was not in a position to judge of the internal economy of the House of Commons, as he had not been there for more than twenty years, and he lived in such Olympian seclusion that it was common report he did not know some of the members of his own Government by sight.

The young Tories believed in Goschen for reasons already given, but the party would not have been led by him. Goschen possessed *some* of the qualities required for a House of Commons leader, but he lacked two that are indispensable. In Mr. Smith's absence he had at this time frequently led the House, and he did not lead it happily. It is the first function of a leader to get the business transacted as smoothly and expeditiously as possible.

Against the featherbed of W. H. Smith's inarticulate placidity Irishmen and Radicals hurled themselves in vain. That good, easy man kept his eye on the clock, and made no speeches, and it was wonderful how he got things through. Goschen was a bar of white-hot iron, that under blows emitted sparks. Instead of laying difficulties, he raised them; and it was curious that, though he scrupulously avoided personalities, his speeches acted on the Opposition as a strong provocative. "I don't mind what you say, but I can't stand that fellow Goschen," Harcourt scribbled on a note which he tossed across the table to Mr. Balfour.

Goschen had another defect as a leader. There never was a public man more deficient in the knack of grappling men to his side with hooks of steel—they trusted him, but it cannot be said they loved him. In private life, among his intimates, I am told that Lord Goschen was delightful, full of humour and gay animal spirits. In the intercourse of the lobbies he was difficult and distant. When he became Member for St. George's, Hanover Square, I, as secretary to the Metropolitan Members, had to apply to him on several matters connected with London business. I found him pompous and unsympathetic, and he seemed to resent being regarded as a Metropolitan Member, or being asked to interest himself in so sectional an affair as the levy of a betterment rate.

The truth is that Goschen was translated too early in life to the Treasury Bench, and never picked up the habit of conversing easily and pleasantly with the rank and file. In 1891 no other leader was possible but Mr. Balfour, then at the zenith of his political career. But it is at least permissible to amuse oneself by speculating what would have been the course of the

Unionist party if Goschen had succeeded Smith as leader. There would probably have been no South African War, and there certainly would have been no Tariff Reform. It is more than likely that there would have been no Education Act on the lines of 1903. How should we have fared?

If Goschen had possessed a little less or a little more of certain qualities, how different might have been the position of the Tory party to-day! We spent our 1900 majority mainly on the business of the parson and the publican, a disinterested expenditure, to be sure, but as a political speculation hardly fortunate. For the parson has turned Socialist, and the publican has lost his influence.

Would Goschen's authority and faculty of rapid decision have saved the party from the disruption of 1903? Mr. Arthur Elliot sums up the services of Goschen to the State in one sentence: " His whole career tended to uphold the character of the life political." That is truly and finely said, though I would expand it a little, and put it higher and more widely. The lesson which Goschen's life bequeaths to the present generation is that there is a loyalty higher, wider, nobler far than the loyalty to a party, namely, loyalty to the laws, the institutions, and the future state of the country of which we are citizens.

Against the pimping politics of the Whips' room Goschen's whole life was a manly and successful protest. He broke with Gladstone, because he thought that Home Rule was wrong. He broke with Chamberlain, because he thought that Tariff Reform was wrong.

Goschen's example is a national possession ; nor, from the lowest point of view, do his courage and independence seem to have been without their reward. For a political life of thirty-seven years, from 1863 to 1900, sixteen were spent as a Cabinet Minister, two were passed as an Ambassador Extraordinary, and the Speakership of the House of Commons and the Viceroyalty of India were offered to him. Not a bad record for one who was

" Too fond of the right to pursue the expedient."

Until the beginning of the century, at all events, it would appear as if gross flattery of the mob, servile adulation of the chief, and secret working of the newspapers, were not the only avenues to power and emolument.

The Balfour-Chamberlain
Partnership

THE RT. HON. JOSEPH CHAMBERLAIN
From Vanity Fair

THE BALFOUR-CHAMBERLAIN PARTNERSHIP

Mr. Balfour was once compelled to address a meeting at Edinburgh and another at Glasgow on the same night, the connection being made by a special train. And then people complain that oratory is obsolete! To make a speech to a mass meeting with a second speech to another meeting hurrying like smoke amongst your ideas is a task which ultimately must break down all but giants or fools. Obviously this hurly-burly was as much beyond Mr. Balfour's strength as it was repugnant to his taste. That is why the man, who in the House of Commons was so easy, so acute, and so brilliant, was too often on the platform a pitiful stammerer of ambiguous generalities.

We must remember that the great men of old days had none of this platform work to do. Chatham never addressed a public meeting in his life. Palmerston spoke about once a year to a village meeting at Tiverton, where his only critic was the butcher. Mr. Balfour was not built in the mould of a Gladstone, or a Bradlaugh, and he simply broke down under the intemperate demands of Demos upon his resources. Apart from his physical inaptitude for mass meetings Mr. Balfour never seemed to have learned that particularity is the essence of oratory, as of poetry.

He was never particular except when pulling an

opponent's argument to pieces in the House of Commons. At public meetings he dealt wholly in general maxims or propositions, of vague and majestic import, but which neither inspired enthusiasm nor carried conviction. It was significant testimony to the declining importance of the House of Commons that Mr. Balfour's dazzling performances in that arena were not considered to atone for his frequent failures on the platform.

Mr. Balfour's retirement from the leadership of the Unionists in 1911 closed an unhappy chapter in the history of the Tory Party, a chapter of indecisions, of blunders, and, consequently, of defeats. It is a chapter that opens with a party strong, united, and victorious, and ends with a party cowed, distracted and exasperated. It would be unfair to debit Mr. Balfour's account with the total loss. The cause of the downfall of the Tory Party was the system of a divided or dual control, which for the ten years (1895 to 1905) was the curse of our counsels.

It is surely one of the grimmest ironies of history that the old Tory Party should have been dealt its mortal stroke by the hand of the late Lord Salisbury. When Lord Randolph Churchill resigned at the end of 1886, Lord Salisbury confided to Mr. Goschen and Lord Hartington that he could not sit in the same Cabinet with Mr. Joseph Chamberlain. Nine years later, in 1895, he invited Mr. Chamberlain to enter his Cabinet, and to bring with him, as members of the Government, a certain number of his friends. Lord

Salisbury's motives in making this offer were probably mixed. He was a generous, and—strange as it may sound to those who only knew him from the outside—an impulsive man.

Doubtless he wished to repay Mr. Chamberlain the debt which he owed for the splendid services of the Radical chief in the defence of the Union. Perhaps he was moved by compassion for the position of cruel and hopeless isolation in which Mr. Chamberlain then stood. It is not unlikely that Lord Salisbury desired, as most Prime Ministers do, to strengthen his party by an alliance. With these motives—and they cannot have been any other—Lord Salisbury took in 1895 the fateful step of forming a Coalition with the Whigs and Radicals who were opposed to Home Rule. Of all the Coalitions in British history, none was fraught with more momentous results to the Tory Party and the Empire.

The Whigs may be dismissed in a sentence. Their position had long been impossible: they were survivals of Palmerstonian days, for whom there was no place in the Liberal Party of 1895. Goschen had already joined the Carlton Club. The Duke of Devonshire subsided into his favourite attitude of acquiescence in the rule of more determined men than himself. He had handed over his political conscience to the keeping of Lord Salisbury instead of Mr. Gladstone, and no doubt he was contented with the change. But with the Birmingham Radicals the case was very different. They were not an old but a new party, and it is proverbially dangerous to put new wine into old bottles.

The Unionist fortress, impregnable as it appeared, was in reality undermined. The Coalition Ministry of 1895, rosy and robust as it seemed to the outer world, harboured within its constitution the germ of disruption. It secured for the Unionists, it is true, a ten years' enjoyment of power, but at the end of that period the party of Bolingbroke, of Pitt, and of Beaconsfield was dispersed for ever.

That the reception of Mr. Joseph Chamberlain *in gremio ecclesiæ* was destined to break up the old Tory connection Lord Salisbury must quickly have realised. Mr. Chamberlain brought with him into the Government a number of relatives and friends, and in the future distribution of appointments he was by no means satisfied with the vast patronage of the Colonial Office, but interfered everywhere to secure the gift of places to Liberal Unionists. Thus not only were a great many Conservatives, who expected and deserved promotion, crowded out of the new Government, but they saw appointment after appointment outside the House of Commons (in India particularly) given to the nominees of Mr. Chamberlain.

The patronage of the party was so handled that to political disappointment was added personal offence. Spurned allegiance and frustrated hopes are strong factors of disintegration in any political party. There was another dissolvent force at work. It was remarkable that Mr. Chamberlain, after accepting office from

Lord Salisbury, never thought it necessary to recant any of his previous Radical opinions about the disestablishment of the Church, the disablement of the House of Lords, and the payment of " ransom " by rich to poor. He allowed these views to sleep; but whenever he was taunted with them by his former allies, he never disowned them, and generally reaffirmed them with some affectation of jocularity.

As Mr. Chamberlain's tenets were shared by his friends in the Government, Conservative views became unfashionable. They were not exactly tabooed; but it was well understood that they were not to be talked about. And thus began the leavening of the lump of Toryism with political infidelity. Then came the electrification of the Colonial Office by its new chief. Lord Salisbury once said that Mr. Gladstone " grasped the sceptre of empire as if it burned his fingers." Mr. Chamberlain brandished it as if he meant to knock somebody on the head.

Very soon, as we remember, the sceptre descended on the crest of Mr. Kruger, and the rap cost us a trifle of two hundred and fifty millions and the importation of Chinese coolies. Lord Salisbury retired in 1902, and died shortly afterwards, when the fatal, accursed duality of leadership, the source of all our misfortunes, began to work. From that dual control, what intrigues, what heartburnings, what humiliations followed! It was not that Mr. Balfour and Mr. Chamberlain were conscious rivals, or that they were insincere in their professions of loyalty and respect for one another. Quite the reverse. The very fact that the two men really liked and respected one another caused the mischief. It was Mr. Chamberlain's loyalty to Mr. Balfour that made him acquiesce in the Education Act of 1902, which must have been very distasteful to him. It was Mr. Balfour's respect for Mr. Chamberlain that prevented him from stopping what he must have known to be the premature and ill-considered projection of Tariff Reform.

If Mr. Chamberlain had been sole leader of the Unionist Party, we should have had no Education Act, or a very different one from that of 1902. If Mr. Balfour had been sole leader, we should have had no campaign for Tariff Reform in the name of the Conservative Party. Two men of first-rate ability, each with his own ideas, and each with his own following, tugging in different directions, must break up the strongest party that ever sat at Westminster.

This is not the place to enter at large upon the Education Act of 1902. The so-called Education Question is really one of money. If Mr. Balfour had doubled or trebled the Imperial grants to the denominational schools, there would have been no Education Question. But Mr. Balfour was so ignorant of the circumstances of the lower-middle class that he did not know that the rate-notes are one of the real troubles of their lives. His argument that there was no difference in principle between rates and Imperial taxes (which few middle-class people pay directly) was ludicrously inept. The result of his Bill was to stir the dregs of a dogged fanaticism as they had not been stirred since Catholic Emancipation, and to crowd the House of Commons elected in 1906 with Dissenters, many of them actually divines. Yet, as a result of the dual control, Mr. Joseph Chamberlain supported the Bill!

When one compares the powerful and compact position of the Conservative party after the rejection of Mr. Gladstone's second Home Rule Bill by the House of Lords in 1895 with its condition in 1906, it is impossible to repress indignation at the long series of blunders and follies committed by Unionist statesmen during that period. The late Lord Salisbury must bear his share of the blame. The Coalition of 1895 was a political mistake of the first order. Except on the government of Ireland it would be difficult to name a single political question on which Mr. Chamberlain and his friends agreed with Lord Salisbury and the Tory Party.

Lord Randolph Churchill excited great wrath amongst the wirepullers by advising the Tories to use the Liberal Unionists as a crutch. The crutch soon became a rod, as the events in South Africa proved. Even the fear of Lord Salisbury, the only man of whom Mr. Chamberlain stood in awe, did not prevent him from dragging the Tory Party into the mistakes of his South African policy. The first fruit of the Coalition was the Transvaal War.

Upon the retirement of Lord Salisbury in 1902 the Birmingham wing of the Coalition no doubt hoped and believed that the leadership would fall to Mr. Chamberlain. The superior claims of the Tory leader, however, were indisputable. And then began the fatal test of Mr. Balfour's character.

Mr. Chamberlain saw that the days of the Dukes were over; he saw it more clearly than his new political partners, for how could Mr. Chaplin and Mr. Balfour be expected to see it? He also saw on the horizon the dawn of the day of democracy. He thought—and this was his first miscalculation—that the Irish question was settled; that Home Rule was dead. The basis of the Unionist Coalition was therefore gone, and something must be found to take its place. " A cry, a cry, my kingdom for a cry!" Then Mr. Chamberlain made his second miscalculation: he thought that Tariff Reform would be just the cry to capture the new democracy.

It was very natural that Mr. Chamberlain should fall into this mistake. He had chosen for himself the post of Secretary of State for the Colonies, and he was full of the Colonies and their politics. The persons whom he was seeing every day were the Agents-General, the Commissioners, and the Prime Ministers of the Colonies. All these people talk Protection hard, naturally enough. Then Mr. Chamberlain had connected himself by the nearest of ties with the United States. In short, the Colonial Secretary lived in the New World, talked its language, shared its aspirations, and ended by convincing himself that its politics (which are nothing but tariffs) must be embraced by the rising British democracy.

The mistake was not only natural, but, in a statesman of Mr. Chamberlain's eager and sympathetic temperament, almost unavoidable. But what of M Balfour ? There was no reason why he should " catch the strong contagion " of the Colonies. Nor did he, as we may judge by Mr. George Peel's narrative,* which, though unfriendly, even a little spiteful, is not inaccurate. Mr. Balfour remained so cool that he froze the hearts of both Free Traders and Protectionists. The quarrel between the two sections of the Unionist Party began immediately after the war. Sir Michael Hicks-Beach had imposed as a war-tax a duty of 2s. a quarter on corn. Sir Michael retired owing to a temporary failure of health, and was succeeded by Mr. Ritchie as Chancellor of the Exchequer, who brought in the Budget of 1903. The majority of the Cabinet were in favour of continuing the 2s. duty on corn in order to enable Mr. Ritchie to make reductions in direct and indirect taxation. Mr. Chamberlain said that unless the 2s. duty were remitted, in whole or in part, on Colonial wheat, he would not have the 2s. duty and would resign if it was persisted in.

The Free Trade members of the Cabinet said that this was a change in the fiscal policy for which the consent of the country must be obtained. As Mr. Chamberlain would not have the 2s. duty without preference, and as the Free Trade members of the Cabinet, headed by the Chancellor of the Exchequer, would not have it with preference, the duty was

* *The Tariff Reformers*, by the Hon. George Peel. London : Methuen.

dropped. Mr. Balfour in this dispute appeared to be on the side of the Free Traders, for he tartly told a deputation which Mr. Chaplin introduced to protest against the dropping of the duty, that untaxed imports of corn were part of the fixed fiscal policy of this country and could only be changed by an express mandate from the electors.

If Mr. Balfour thought that Mr. Ritchie, Lord Balfour of Burleigh, and Lord George Hamilton had " downed " Mr. Chamberlain, he was soon undeceived. Mr. Chamberlain consulted his caucus, counted his boroughs, and resigned. Mr. Balfour kept back Mr. Chamberlain's letter of resignation for two days; and before it was read to the Cabinet, the Free Trade members, thinking the relations with Mr. Chamberlain uncomfortable, resigned. This transaction is certainly one of the most extraordinary in politics.

Mr. Chamberlain retired because the majority of the Cabinet were opposed to his fiscal policy, and because he wished to have a free hand for " the tearing, raging campaign." But, in withdrawing, Mr. Chamberlain managed to draw out with himself the three leading Free Trade Tories of the Cabinet, Lord Balfour of Burleigh, Lord George Hamilton, and Mr. Ritchie, and to replace them by three Liberal Unionist Tariff Reformers, Mr. Austen Chamberlain, Mr. Alfred Lyttelton, and Mr. Arnold Forster.

The Chancellor of the Exchequer is, of course, the Minister who holds the key of the financial policy of a Cabinet. Mr. Ritchie, the Free Trader, was allowed by

The Balfour-Chamberlain Partnership

Mr. Balfour to retire; and Mr. Chamberlain was allowed by Mr. Balfour to put his son in his place. This affair is the more astonishing because there is no doubt that at that time Mr. Balfour was on the side of the Free Traders. But, in vulgar parlance, Mr. Chamberlain " walked round " Mr. Balfour : from the Birmingham point of view, the reconstruction of the Balfour Cabinet was a master-stroke.

It cut deep into the minds of observant Tories. Mr. Winston Churchill, looking about to see who might be his future leader, folded his tent swiftly and fled to the enemy's camp, whither he was followed by Colonel Seely, Sir John Dickson Poynder, Sir George Kemp, and many others in the country. The Duke of Devonshire, whom a vain attempt to placate was made by taking his son-in-law, Lord Stanley, into the Cabinet, slowly and reluctantly left Mr. Balfour to be dealt with by the Birmingham gang. The process of walking round Mr. Balfour was continued for the next seven years, at a steadily accelerated pace. The pen of Mr. George Peel has tracked Mr. Balfour's doublings and backings, and twistings and turnings, with a zeal which must satisfy the most malignant Radical. It is painful reading: and yet one is tempted to ask, whose fault was it but Mr. Balfour's ?

And what really was in Mr. Balfour's mind all the while ? When he formed his Government in 1902 Mr. Balfour's authority was unchallenged : he had only to maintain it. By lifting his little finger he could have stopped the persecution of the Free Trade Conservatives, which was prompted by Birmingham, and eagerly carried on by those insects of intrigue, the " Confederates." Yet Mr. Balfour made no effort to save Mr. George Bowles at Norwood, or Lord Robert Cecil at Marylebone, or Lord Hugh Cecil at Greenwich, or Mr. Gibson Bowles at Kings Lynn. He folded his arms and said, " Persecution is not my job : I leave it to others." But what really was in Mr. Balfour's mind ? He kept on repeating : " I am a Tariff Reformer ; the first plank in our constructive platform is Tariff Reform." Yet he stolidly refused to discuss a question, whose essence is detail.

Some of his friends declared that Mr. Balfour was mentally incapable of handling figures. But this is absurd. Some men have a natural liking and facility for figures. Others dislike them and handle them only by an effort. Any educated man can deal with figures if he chooses to take the trouble. It is not to be supposed that Disraeli had any natural aptitude for figures ; as a literary man he probably disliked them. Yet when he fought Sir Robert Peel in 1846 he made long statistical speeches in the House of Commons, dealing with imports and exports and percentages as deftly as any professor of the London School of Economics.

When he introduced his Budget, in 1852, Disraeli spoke for three hours and astonished the House of Commons by his easy mastery of the necessary arithmetic. It is ridiculous to tell us that a statesman who has written the *Defence of Philosophic Doubt,* and who analyses Bergson, could not use the Statistical Abstract of the Board of Trade. It is, of course, possible that Mr. Balfour did not choose to take the trouble of getting up figures. But it is hardly probable that the leader of a great party was guilty of what in a company director would be deemed *crassa negligentia, quæ dolo equiparatur*.

The more likely explanation is that Mr. Balfour deliberately came to the conclusion that the best means of " keeping the party together "—that phrase so dear to the heart of a Whip !—was to seem to agree with Jew and Gentile, to be all things to all men as long as possible. If so, the miscalculation was as grave as Mr. Chamberlain's talk of ruined industries and decaying trades.

Mr. Balfour's calculated inanity satisfied neither the Protectionists nor the Free Traders, and excited the distrust of both. But the mischief was slight so long as it was confined to the delivery of sonorous and elusive generalities on Primrose platforms. Empty, disappointed, and perplexed, these audiences went away, wondering on what Mr. Balfour's great House of Commons reputation rested. These exhibitions were dull, but not dangerous. The real danger arose when Mr. Balfour and Lord Lansdowne allowed themselves to be persuaded or bullied by the Tariff Reformers into using the House of Lords as a weapon in the party game. By 1909, as Mr. Peel has shown, the Tariff Reformers had subdued Mr. Balfour to a proper frame of mind.

The proposals which aroused the fiercest animosity against the Budget of 1909 amongst the Tories in the House of Commons were the super-tax, the undeveloped land duty, and the tax on unearned increment. It was quite natural that taxes such as these should exasperate the class which owns money and land; and quite right that these taxes should be opposed in the House of Commons and criticised in the House of Lords. But as we know that 90 per cent. of the electors do not pay income-tax or death duties, was it not madness on the part of the 10 per cent. to appeal to the 90 per cent. to let them off by substituting duties on food-stuffs and commodities?

The real issue of the first general election of 1910 was this: Shall the money for old age pensions and insurance and dreadnoughts be supplied by duties on meat, wheat, dairy produce, and foreign manufactures? Or shall it be found by taxing the landlords and financiers? Angry as the Lords naturally were, it is not credible that, if left to themselves, they would have forced an appeal to the country on such an issue, for the Peers are men of the world, and not being professional politicians, generally take a saner view of a crisis than House of Commons leaders.* But the Tariff Reformers had got hold of Mr. Balfour and Lord Lansdowne; and the habit of discipline, or the spirit of gambling, prevailed.

If we lose the election, some peers argued, we cannot

* Lord Oxford has told us in his *Fifty Years* that his Cabinet was divided upon these taxes, and that a section was in favour of dropping them.

be worse off than we are; and if we win, Ireland, the Church, the Crown, our own order, the land, all are saved. It was another miscalculation, for the election was lost, and the one after that, and the peers found themselves a great deal worse off than before.

The results of rejecting the Budget of 1909 were the degradation of the Royal prerogative, and the destruction of the ancient House of Lords. It is Mr. George Peel's judgment that the two adverse elections of 1910 and the Parliament Act completed Mr. Balfour's ruin as a party leader, and decided him to retire. I do not dispute Mr. Peel's proposition, but observe that the two elections of 1910 were the work of the Tariff Reformers.

It is difficult to see what other course compatible with dignity Mr. Balfour could have taken. The power of the House of Lords was obviously his last resource; he had used it at the wrong time, and it had broken in his hands. What was left to him unless he began life anew as a platform teacher of elementary economics? With wisdom and dignity, the statesman who had defeated Parnell and the Land League left that job to other and younger hands. After a hurried comparison of the qualities of Mr. Walter Long and Mr. Austen Chamberlain, a candidate appeared who had sat for less than a dozen years in the House of Commons, who had filled a subordinate office for three years, but who had thoroughly mastered the details of Tariff Reform.

Mr. Bonar Law was appointed leader of the Tory

Party by the Tariff Reformers, who within a few months decided that the names of Tory and Conservative must be deleted for ever. As Disraeli said to John Bright, in an upper-chamber in Grosvenor Gate, with the candour of the dressing-gown, "That infernal question of Protection!"

Mr. Peel accuses Mr. Balfour of deciding to accept Mr. Chamberlain's policy, and at the same time of resolving not to act upon it. This is really the gravamen of the charge against his leadership. Only those who do not understand the difficulties of the tariff question would blame a statesman for hesitating to make up his mind about Free Trade and Protection. Rénan compared the human consciousness to a lighthouse with revolving fires. Now the lanthorn whirls round to the economic sandbank; and now it flashes upon the moral and political rocks. Commercial restriction might be economically indefensible, and yet in certain conditions it might be morally, and therefore politically, justifiable.

The statesman is not to consider only the acquisition and distribution of wealth, he must attend to national character and national defence. Fiscal protection, like conscription, might be costly; but it might be worth the cost; and it would then become the statesman's duty to convince his countrymen, by earnest and energetic teaching, that it was worth the cost. Thoughtful men, both in business and in politics, would have praised instead of blaming Mr. Balfour if he had said: "I am unable to make up my mind about Tariff

Reform ; I insist upon its being treated as an open question, like female suffrage ; and I will not allow the party organisation to be used to crush out those Conservatives who have not been converted by the Birmingham sect."

Mr. Balfour accepted Tariff Reform from Mr. Chamberlain as the main constructive policy of the Unionist Party but obstinately refused to say what he meant by it. He thus allowed his supporters to flounder about at elections while he kept a free hand to give whatever meaning he chose, or might think ultimately expedient, to the words. This was opportunism carried to the depth of cynicism, and accompanied as it was by Mr. Balfour's perfect indifference to the natural hunger of all parties for honours and rewards, it is not surprising that his followers murmured. After being Prime Minister since 1902 and leader of the House of Commons since 1891, Mr. Balfour resigned office in 1905 without bestowing a title, or a ribbon, or a pension, or an office, on any of his supporters, except his brother and his private secretary.

It is historically interesting to sum up exactly what the Tariff Reformers did to the Tory Party in the decade between 1903 and 1913. (1) They drove out of Mr. Balfour's Government Mr. Ritchie, Lord George Hamilton, Lord Balfour of Burleigh, and the Duke of Devonshire. (2) They drove out of the Conservative party Mr. Winston Churchill and General Seely. (3) They drove out of Parliament Lord Robert and Lord

Hugh Cecil,* Mr. Thomas Gibson Bowles, his son, Mr. George Bowles, and Mr. Harold Cox. (4) They lost three general elections. (5) They procured the rejection of the Budget of 1909 with its consequence, the destruction of the House of Lords.

Such has been the result of the combined statesmanship of Mr. Chamberlain and Mr. Balfour. History, when she pays her tribute to the virtues of these two great men, will be forced to record that they disunited, and for a time dissolved, the party which had shared with its rival the noble and perilous duties of government for over two hundred years.

The rejection by the House of Lords of Mr. Lloyd George's Budget in 1909 was the last trump of Lord Lansdowne and Mr. Balfour, egged on by the Tariff Reformers, and they found themselves overtrumped by the Government. The first of the two elections sealed with the electors' approval a Finance Act, many of whose clauses were afterwards repealed by the Government of which their author was the head. The second election in the same year, while it left the Government with a majority much reduced from that of 1905, gave it a vague mandate for curtailing the powers of the House of Lords, which issued in the Parliament Act of 1911. It is not surprising that Mr. Balfour chose this moment to resign the leadership of the Unionist Party, though the reason which he gave to his constituents in the City of London is, in the light of subsequent events, remarkable. Mr. Balfour told

*Happily in the case of Lord Salisbury's sons the exclusion was only temporary.

his friends that there came an age when a man's mental power began to contract, and he was anxious to retire before that happened to him! From 1911 to the outbreak of Armageddon Mr. Balfour was *functus officio*, though in the summer of 1914 he appeared as an elder statesman in the Buckingham Palace councils on Home Rule.

It is beyond the scope of this book to give an account of the marvellous summer of St. Martin which gilded the second career of Lord Balfour as a Minister during the Great War. Its facile and felicitous course illustrates the view I have always taken of this statesman's character, namely, that he was greater as a man of action, than as a thinker or a manager of men. In the first war coalition of 1915, Mr. Balfour became First Lord of the Admiralty; and in the second coalition, formed by Mr. Lloyd George in 1916, he accepted the post of Foreign Secretary, in which capacity he visited the United States in 1917 as Head of the British Mission. He made a speech from the floor of the Senate and declared himself a democrat, of course without a big D. Not an eyelid flickered, not a lip twitched among the senators at this audacious flattery of his audience by an impenetrable aristocrat. American courtesy, or credulity, acclaimed the address with enthusiasm, and Mr. Balfour left the indelible impression of an English gentleman, afterwards to be compared with somewhat different types of British negotiator. An earldom and the Garter crowned the second youth of Lord Balfour in 1922.

If I have not painted the latter years with more minuteness, it is because this chapter is not a commentary on Lord Balfour's life—had it been so I should have dwelt on his superb achievement as Chief Secretary for Ireland in the last century—but a criticism of his Premiership from 1902 to 1905, and his leadership of the Opposition from 1906 to 1911.

Open questions are nearly always fatal to Governments, and I must add a few final words on that open question of fiscal policy, which excluded the Tory Party from power for nearly twenty years and is not settled yet.

The guns of the Great War have blown the theory of Free Trade (along with many other theories) to atoms. I have always held that for a society in an advanced stage of development the theory of free exchange is unassailable and the theory of protection indefensible. But all economic theories, like the deductions in mathematics, rest on postulates. Free exchange is based on the assumption that peace will be maintained between the Great Powers. And after fifty years of commercial prosperity, the philosophers and economists of the transition period became the victims of the illusion out of which Mr. Norman Angell made his reputation, namely, that war was so ruinous that it could not occur.

The mistake made by the Tariff Reformers was that they rested their case on economic, instead of on moral and political grounds. Instead of saying boldly, " It is dangerous to rely so largely on foreign supplies of food, we must subsidise agriculture ; and it is madness to be absolutely dependent on Germany for chemicals, spelter, sugar, and dyes, we must protect those trades at home " ; they muddled themselves and their audiences with absurd calculations to prove that more money would be made by Tariff Reform than by Free Exchange.

The war has made some measure of Protection inevitable. But how much stronger the position of the Tariff Reformers would have been if they had taken the moral and political instead of the economic ground ! Disraeli opposed the repeal of the Corn Laws in 1846, not upon economic grounds, but because the maintenance of the landed interest was of prime social and political importance. He called upon all ranks of society to consent, if necessary, to pay more for their bread in order to save agriculture from extinction.

To quote the eloquent words of Professor Hearnshaw in his essay on Disraeli in *The Prime Minister of the Nineteenth Century,* " He fought for the menaced farm against the encroaching factory ; for the vanishing village against the spreading slum ; for the cause of agriculture against the industrial revolution." This is very different from Chamberlain's exhibition of two loaves from under the table with the assurance to the Birmingham artisans that the protection loaf was no smaller or dearer than the Free Trade one. And was not Disraeli splendidly right in 1846, as he always was ?

Lord Randolph Churchill

LORD RANDOLPH CHURCHILL
Elliott and Fry

LORD RANDOLPH CHURCHILL

MUCH has been written about Lord Randolph Churchill, naturally, as he was one of the most original and attractive figures of the last century. He has been more fortunate than other great men in his biographers. Lord Chesterfield's character has come down to us enveloped in the angry words of Dr. Johnson and his reporter Boswell. Halifax the Trimmer, quite the most charming and cultured character of the seventeenth century, is passed on to us by Bishop Burnet as a fribble and an atheist. Lord Randolph has, as his recorders, his son and a sympathetic friend, Lord Rosebery.

Apart from its intrinsic merits, which are great, Mr. Winston Churchill's Life of his father* is invested with an adventitious interest by the fact that he wrote it as a member of the Conservative Party and published it as a member of the Liberal Party. With future events germinating in his mind Mr. Churchill writes on page 448 (the chapter on the Parnell Commission): " But let it be observed that Lord Randolph Churchill was beaten, whatever he did, when he played the national game, and was victorious, whatever he did, while he played the party game. No question of ' taste' or ' patriotism ' was raised when what he said, however outrageous, suited his party. No claim of truth

*Life of Lord Randolph Churchill, by Winston Spencer Churchill. 2 Vols. Macmillan.

counted when what he said, however incontrovertible, was awkward for his party."

He was that familiar figure in history since the days of Alcibiades, an aristocrat with strong democratic sympathies. He was vehemently anti-Jingo in foreign politics, and as early as 1877 tried to get up an intrigue with Sir Charles Dilke against Lord Beaconsfield's Turkish policy, actually offering to propose in the House of Commons the establishment of republics in Bulgaria and Herzegovina! In Egyptian politics he supported Wilfrid Blunt and Arabi Pacha, and in short was the champion of " oppressed nationalities." In home politics Lord Randolph Churchill was frankly Radical, favouring graduated taxation and enfranchisement of leaseholds.

All this he called Tory Democracy ; the democracy was plain enough, but where was the Toryism ? Lord Randolph would have been happier, and more successful, if he had joined the Radical Party before 1880. Had he adhered to Mr. Gladstone in 1886 ; he would certainly have been his successor. If he had gone with Mr. Chamberlain and Lord Hartington, his position as a Radical Unionist would have been unassailable. But Lord Randolph Churchill's environment was too much for him. His defection to the Radicals would have been a grievous blow to those whom he loved and wished to please

Once he broke out when his father was Viceroy of Ireland in an anti-coercionist speech (1877), and the Duke of Marlborough wrote to the Chief Secretary :

"My dear Beach—The only excuse I can find for Randolph is, that he must either be mad, or have been singularly affected with local champagne or claret." Towards the end of his life Lord Randolph was fond of saying, "I don't believe in dooks; I've seen too much of 'em." But at the beginning of his life the ducal influence was strong. When the Duke of Marlborough died in 1883 Lord Randolph was in the full swing of his opposition to the Gladstonian Government, and three years later came the Home Rule Bill.

It is the old story of missed opportunity. Meditating deeply on all these things, as the drama of his father's life unfolded itself beneath his eyes, Mr. Churchill determined not to miss his opportunity. He deserved not blame but praise for his decision to leave, before it was too late, a party with which he was in imperfect sympathy. Twenty years later, with equal courage and greater prescience, he has repeated the operation. As a frank soldier of fortune he is without a rival. His fluent allegiance resembles that of no other character in history so closely as John, first Duke of Marlborough. Nothing would surprise me less than the discovery that he is in secret correspondence with his exiled Sovereign in Cheyne Walk.

The highest point in Lord Randolph's political life was touched, in my opinion, between 1880 and 1885, when he was beating down Mr. Gladstone in the House of Commons, and building up the Tory party in the big towns. Mr. Gladstone had emerged from the Midlothian campaign with a halo of glory such as never before or since surrounded the head of statesman. Gladstone-worship was rampant, and Lord Randolph Churchill was determined to break it down. Events favoured his enterprise, for never was Prime Minister so unlucky as Mr. Gladstone.

It was a strange trick of fortune that a man of Mr. Gladstone's intense piety and scholarly refinement should have been compelled to throw the ægis of his eloquence over a blatant atheist like Bradlaugh. Bradlaugh was the foundation-stone of the Fourth Party, which found plenty of work for its hands in South Africa, in Egypt, and in Ireland. A peace-loving Minister, who detested foreign and colonial politics of every description, found himself dragged into a South African war ending in Majuba Hill; into Egyptian complications involving the suppression of Arabi, the bombardment of Alexandria, the abortive Soudan disaster, the mission and murder of Gordon, and into a species of civil war with Parnell and the Land League in Ireland.

Not a single point escaped Lord Randolph Churchill, and with the eye of a born tactician, he so selected his topics of attack that he managed to enlist a certain amount of Radical support for his most furious onslaughts on the Government. At the same time he waged a kind of left-handed war against his own leader in the House of Commons, Sir Stafford Northcote. It is a most interesting historical fact that Lord Beaconsfield confided to Sir John Gorst that he would never have taken a peerage and left Sir Stafford Northcote to lead the House of Commons, if he had not believed that Mr. Gladstone meant what he said when he announced his retirement in 1874.

That Lord Randolph's treatment of Sir Stafford Northcote was marked by brutality cannot be gainsaid. Disraeli's attacks on Sir Robert Peel were also brutal. Men climb to the topmost place in politics on the bodies of their comrades. As the first Lord Halifax observed, " State business is a cruel trade ; good nature is a bungler in it." The capture of the " machine," the National Union of Conservative Associations, completed Lord Randolph Churchill's triumph over the " old gang " or " the goats," as the Fourth Party nicknamed that trio of worthies, Sir Stafford Northcote, Sir Richard Cross, and Mr. W. H. Smith. At the same time the brilliant guerilla chief became the idol of provincial platforms.

Lord Randolph's speech at Blackburn in 1884 (the " chips " speech) will bear comparison with some of Disraeli's happiest exhibitions of satire and invective. This was the greatest period of Lord Randolph Churchill's career. He was the Conservative Party of that hour. When Conservatism was fast degenerating into old fogeyism and fat obstruction, Lord Randolph rehabilitated it by his own genius, breathed into its nostrils the breath of a popular movement, and made it a victorious force in the workshops of the artisans. If the borough franchise had not been extended to the agricultural labourers in 1884 there can be no doubt that the Conservatives would have swept the board in 1885, and, as it was, they captured the big towns, driving the Radicals into Bœotia. Strong as was the national feeling against Home Rule, I do not believe that the Unionist majority in 1886 would have been anything like so large had it not been for Lord Randolph Churchill's conquest of the centres of industry between 1880 and 1885.

His abiding title to a place among statesmen is that he made Conservatism popular with the working classes, as only Disraeli had done before, and as possibly no one will ever do again. "Lord Randy," as the working men used to call him, was very popular with the masses.

Between the highest and the lowest class there is what Thackeray called a " common bond of blackguardism." The middle class is regarded as an enemy by both. Suddenly in 1885 the successful rebel was converted into a suave and dignified Secretary of State for India, a post which he held for six months. We have Sir Arthur Godley's testimony that Lord Randolph was one of the best Secretaries of State who ever ruled the India Office. And I can easily believe it, for he was industrious, and far too clever not to know what he did not know. Nothing distinguishes a first-rate from a second-rate man more sharply than the former's trust in skilled subordinates as contrasted with the latter's fussy suspicions.

After the election of 1886 Lord Randolph Churchill became Chancellor of the Exchequer and Leader of the House of Commons. Although the autumn session of that year was too short a time to test his real quality, Lord Randolph led with dignity, firmness and courtesy. His knowledge of the world enabled him to manage a mixed assembly, and although he sometimes rebuked a follower in private rather roughly, in the House he was conciliation itself. It was in December that the crash came. The crux of the situation was that Lord Randolph required the reduction of the Admiralty and War Office estimates by £1,300,000.

Mr. W. H. Smith and Lord George Hamilton, in the most friendly and argumentative letters, wrote that they could not see their way to being responsible for the reductions demanded. Lord Salisbury was of course appealed to, and while negotiations were still in progress, the Chancellor of the Exchequer wrote from Windsor Castle on 20th December, 1886, to the Prime Minister, tendering his resignation, which Lord Salisbury accepted on the 22nd, and on the 23rd the news was in the *Times*. Even at the time Lord Randolph's friends were aghast, and he received an extremely sensible letter of advice from Mr. Labouchere, in which the following sentence occurs : " I should have thought that your game was rather a waiting one. Sacrifice everything to becoming a fetish : then, and only then, you can do as you like."

But to wait and submit himself to others were the two things Lord Randolph Churchill was temperamentally incapable of doing ; and from the day when the world discovered this fact it turned its back on him. Other Ministers have resigned and increased their popularity; but Lord Randolph lost a great deal more than office: he parted with the confidence of men. He made two miscalculations of so gross a character as to be almost unintelligible. He thought himself indispensable, and he believed economy to be popular in practice, whereas it is only popular in theory.

After his resignation Lord Randolph Churchill made several good speeches from his corner seat behind the Treasury bench, and on one great question he was indisputably right and the Government wrong. The appointment of the Parnell Commission was unconstitutional and impolitic. It is a sound maxim that an extraordinary tribunal should never be set up to try an issue which could be tried by the ordinary courts. As a political move it was a gross blunder, because the Unionists would have gained more by taunting Parnell with his fear of a British jury than they gained by the report of the judges, which produced no result, as it was too long to read.

The election of 1892 threw the Conservatives into Opposition, and drew them together again. Lord Randolph Churchill was once more received into favour and resumed his seat on the Front Bench. But it was too late. The speech on the disestablishment of the Welsh Church was the last leap of a dying fire. The blithe and debonair Lord Randolph was transformed at forty-five into a paralytic dotard, struggling heroically with a pitiless Até. His friends and relatives were unable to prevent him making platform speeches: " but the crowds who were drawn by the old glamour of his name departed sorrowful and shuddering at the spectacle of a dying man, and those who loved him were consumed with embarrassment and grief." In these words Mr. Churchill describes one of the most tragic ends in history.

Lord Rosebery's little book on Lord Randolph Churchill is by far the most interesting production of his pen. It is written in a more easy and colloquial style than his Pitt or Buonaparte—the hero, for instance, is referred to throughout as " Randolph." But what this monograph lacks in care and polish is more than made up for by its spontaneity, and by the vital interest of Lord Rosebery's comments on the political parties of his own day, and on a career which has some striking points of resemblance to his own. Lord Randolph Churchill was a brilliant half-success, because an aristocrat by birth, a Tory by tradition, he was at heart a Radical.

" *Mutato nomine de te fabula narratur.*" Lord Rosebery is an aristocrat to his finger tips, a Whig by heredity, and at heart a Tory. Both Lord Randolph Churchill and Lord Rosebery were born in the wrong party, and neither had the strength of mind to change. For Lord Rosebery in the cynicism of his experience behind the scenes, compares the two front benches to opposing counsel in a big case of which the public is judge. The difference is that counsel avowedly speak from their briefs, while politicians profess to speak from their convictions.

But Lord Randolph Churchill's failure was not wholly due to the fact that he was a Radical among Tories : it was largely due to his uncontrollable temper, aggravated after 1886 by the malady which killed him. With the exception of Lord Salisbury, whom he teased with unreasonable letters couched in pompous language, there was probably no one of his colleagues whom he had not insulted.* Such a person, be his genius never so transcendent, is shortly summed up by practical men as " impossible."

Lord Rosebery subjects Tory Democracy to a scathing analysis, bluntly describing it as " an imposture." This is not quite fair. It is true that there is no discoverable connection between Tory Democracy and the principles of Lord Beaconsfield, as is commonly supposed. Disraeli, like George III, was bent on breaking the power of the Whigs, whom he spoke and wrote of as " the Venetian oligarchy." Like Bolingbroke, he nursed the idea of a Sovereign who should govern as well as reign. He also believed in the influence of the Church and the aristocracy, if exercised socially upon the masses.

These were the political ideas on which Disraeli traded as novelist and politician during the earlier

* Lord George Hamilton, in his Recollections, hints that Lord Randolph was involved in some disreputable scandal and resigned in the fear of blackmail. There is no evidence whatever to support this suggestion, which, had it been true, would surely have resulted in the disappearance of Lord Randolph, for the time being at all events, from the House of Commons, and probably from the country. But, on the contrary, he remained, not only in London Society, but in his place in the House of Commons after his resignation.

part of his life. On the shoulders of Lord George Bentinck and the Protectionist squires he climbed into office, and when there, very sensibly dropped Protection. When at the close of his life Disraeli acceded to real power in 1874, " Young England " ideas were the dreams of boyhood; but discerning the Jingo instincts of the newly enfranchised artisans he went in for " a spirited foreign policy." Anything more unlike Lord Randolph's Tory Democracy than the idealism of Disraeli's earlier years, or the imperialism of his later years, cannot be imagined.

Randolph Churchill hated Jingoism, and in domestic politics he adopted the bold, if simple expedient of cribbing the views of extreme Radicals. His celebrated Dartford speech was merely an animated *réchauffé* of the violent reforms of all the Radical faddists of the day. Mr. Chamberlain, his personal friend, and never an unkindly critic, said that Lord Randolph Churchill had " borrowed from the cast-off policy of all the extreme men of all the different sections. He took his Socialism from Mr. Burns and Mr. Hyndman; he took his local option from Sir Wilfrid Lawson; he took his Egyptian policy from Mr. Illingworth; he took his metropolitan reform from Mr. Stewart; and he took his Irish policy from Mr. John Morley. Is this Toryism ?" There was too much truth in this sally, except as regards Ireland, for on the subject of Home Rule Lord Randolph was always staunch, though he undoubtedly bargained away a Coercion Bill for the sake of the Irish vote in 1885.

It is not difficult to understand why the idol of his party became its terror the moment he tried his hand at constructive statesmanship.

Lord Rosebery is unstinted in his praise of Randolph Churchill's oratory, though naturally he never heard him speak on the platform. Lord Randolph shared with Gladstone, Bright and Chamberlain the distinction of being equally successful in the House of Commons and at a public meeting. Lord Beaconsfield very seldom attempted to address monster meetings, being well aware of his physical limitations; when he was obliged to do so, as at the Crystal Palace and the Pomona Gardens, Manchester, he spoke to the reporters. Lord Salisbury was painfully cold and awkward on the platform, the shy academic all over. But Randolph Churchill was in his element at a big boisterous meeting, to which he came fully prepared with every kind of rhetorical entertainment, the solemn exordium, the violent personal abuse of opponents, the genial jokes, and then the solemn peroration. A speaker cannot prepare too elaborately for a public meeting, which will well repay his trouble. Randolph Churchill used to write his speeches out in full, read them over two or three times, make copious notes, and then deliver them with great dramatic ease and force, as if he was pouring out profuse and unpremeditated thoughts. This is a wonderful gift, and possessed by most really great public speakers. Brougham, Bright, and Disraeli possessed it, as did Chamberlain. Gladstone's speeches were too diffuse to be written ; and Lord Salisbury did not write—it would have been better if he had ; nor did Mr. Balfour.

For the House of Commons Lord Randolph prepared quite as carefully, but in a different vein, remembering Disraeli's dictum, *Paradise Lost* for the House of Lords, *Don Juan* for the House of Commons. Randolph's speeches in the House of Commons were pointed and eloquent conversation, the wit and *insouciance* of a finished man of the world, with a due admixture of stately phrasing when the occasion called for it. As rhetorical performances I agree with Lord Rosebery that Randolph Churchill's speeches were excellent, though whether they will be good reading fifty years hence it is difficult to say. All old speeches are not dull reading. Disraeli's speeches on the Corn Law are as amusing pieces of literary invective as the Letters of Junius. Some of Brougham's speeches, nearly all Bright's, and Lowe's on Parliamentary reform, are well worth reading as specimens of English composition.

Considering his defective education—for a hunting undergraduate at Merton does not read much*—the literary quality of Randolph Churchill's speeches is surprising, nor do I believe that he was assisted in their composition by his friends, only one of whom

---

* I believe that Gibbon and Macaulay were the only classical writers with whom Lord Randolph had any acquaintance. In the Bradlaugh debate he alluded to "Orīgen, one of the Fathers." Some one behind said "Orĭgen." Lord Randolph dug his heels into the floor and repeated "Orīgen." He was doubtless thinking of "fons et origo mali," a tag with which he was familiar.

indeed was capable of doing so. Some one told me that he was once admitted to see Randolph when he was composing a speech, and found him lying on his stomach on the hearthrug surrounded by sheets of manuscript. On another occasion he had the reporters up to his house in Connaught Place, and recited to them in the morning the speech he was going to make that evening at Bradford or Manchester.

After the delivery of " the rotten, bloody fœtus Pigott " passage in his attack on the Government for appointing the Parnell Commission it was evident that Lord Randolph was suffering, not only from great mental excitement, but from physical exhaustion. His utterance became thick, his voice sank to a hoarse whisper, and his tongue moved along his lips. He turned his back upon the Speaker, and looked helplessly about him, muttered, " Will some one get me a glass of water ? "

A fallen minister has no friends. Not a man of those around him stirred, though a year ago not a man of them but would have flown to do his bidding. I happened to be sitting two benches behind Lord Randolph Churchill, that is, on the fourth bench from the floor, and as soon as I realised that none of those near him would move, I marched down the floor and out into the lobby to the bar. As I returned up the floor bearing a tumbler, I perceived from the cheers which greeted me from the Opposition that I had performed what the French call *un beau geste*. Lord Randolph's hand shook so as he took the glass that I thought he would have spilled the water, and he said, " Thank you, I hope I don't compromise you." Two days later I received the following letter from the venerable Mr. Samuel Plimsoll :

> Dear Sir,—Will you excuse a stranger to you taking the liberty of thanking you very heartily for the courtesy and kindness that you showed to Lord Randolph Churchill in bringing him a glass of water in the House of Commons when so many others refused so simple an act of kindness. You are a Conservative, and so is Lord Randolph Churchill, but we are all three men, and I imagine that not one of us would be guilty of the meanness of the so-called friends of Lord Randolph Churchill.
> I am, dear Sir, yours faithfully,
> SAMUEL PLIMSOLL.
>
> P.S.—I feel sure that a similar feeling of admiration and gratitude to yourself would arise in thousands of other people, even though they do not write to you.—S.P.

On the whole, I cannot see that a case has been made out for Randolph Churchill's ill-treatment by his party. His services to the Conservative cause between 1880 and 1885 were enormous, and they were rewarded by the Chancellorship of the Exchequer and the leadership of the House of Commons. Lord Randolph turned himself out of office, because he could not bend and tutor to his will men of greater experience in administration than himself. It is true that some of the changes which he demanded were afterwards effected by his colleagues. But that only proves that with a little patience and control of temper he might have remained where he was. So that it all comes back to the truth that success depends more on temperament (including health) and character than on ability.

In person Lord Randolph Churchill was slight and fragile, which made him look shorter than he really was. His height was, I believe, five feet nine inches, but he appeared to be shorter. He had protruding, light blue eyes, and in his younger days his face curiously suggested a pugnacious Blenheim spaniel. His voice was strong but not melodious, and his utterance was sometimes marred by a curious sibilation, not exactly a lisp, which disappeared when he was excited. His dress was rather dandified, but always the same—a black bow tie, frock-coat never buttoned, a well-ironed silk hat worn with a slight cock. In the pursuit of pleasure he was reckless to an incredible degree, not caring what people might say, or how his health might be affected.

The beginning of the end was marked, about four years before his death, when he grew a beard, and slouched about in a blue suit. He was nearly always engaged in a violent quarrel with some one of his world, but he was not vindictive. At one time there was a vendetta between the houses of Hamilton and Churchill, and then "that damned fellow George" (First Lord of the Admiralty) was not to be spoken to. Then he fell foul of Mr. Chaplin, and whenever " that fool Harry " rose to address the House, Lord Randolph rose to leave it. One afternoon at the hour of three—

a time usually sacred to the consumption of cigarettes —I found him all alone on the green benches, watching like a cat the member in charge of private business at the table.

" You may wonder why I am here at such an hour," he said ; " this is why I'm here," and he thrust into my hand a private bill for conferring lighting powers on some electrical company, which began with the words, " Whereas the Most Noble George, Duke of Marlborough." I looked puzzled, and so he explained. " That cursed brother of mine thinks he can smuggle any bills he likes through this House. But I'll put a spoke in his wheel." Accordingly he sprang up, and, by objecting, took the bill out of the class of unopposed private business. Probably he had quarrelled with the Most Noble George at the Turf Club on some trumpery issue, which, a week later, he would forget. Such was this strange wayward being, now swayed by the pettiest personal motives, and now soaring with strong and fearless stroke into the region of high politics, where his vision would be keen and calm, his spirit high, and his words inspiring. Lord Randolph Churchill was surely a radiant figure in the dun-coloured array of conventional politicians.

Walter Bagehot

WALTER BAGEHOT

Walter Bagehot (1826-79) was a Palmerstonian Whig, though he called himself a Liberal. His creed, based as it was on fear of the mob, like Gibbon's, I take to be the quintessence of Victorian Toryism, on its temperamental, not political, side. It is interesting to compare it with what passes for Conservatism to-day.

Many literary men—all wise literary men—have made the writing of books a πάρεργον, and have followed some other trade to give them bread and experience. It was the weakness of Johnson and Carlyle that they knew nothing of money and business: it much impaired their influence as preachers, for both talked nonsense about trade. There seems to be something at once soothing and stimulating in the daily contemplation of other people's liabilities, for, amongst bankers, Grote, Lubbock, and Bagehot were placid and prolific writers. Bagehot died at the age of fifty-two, and his manhood divides itself into two decades: the first ten years were spent at Langport and Bristol in learning the trade of bank-manager; during the second ten years he lived in London, and, while managing the metropolitan business of Stuckey's Bank, he was Editor of the *Economist*, occasional editor of the *National Review*, and a contributor to the *Fortnightly* and *Saturday Reviews*. Only they who are impelled by self interest or intellectual curiosity to read or write much about politics are aware of the extent of Bagehot's influence upon the political philosophy of the mid-Victorian age. Like Burke's, it is a saturating influence, often undetected because so seldom acknowledged. Bagehot did for political theory very much what Matthew Arnold and Renan did for Christian theology, and he did it by pretty much the same method. Each of these great writers was in his own province a dissolvent force, working by gentle ridicule and playful argument to explode accepted tradition and to test conventional theories. Thus it is a favourite saying of Bagehot in dealing with the British Constitution : " The books are all wrong: the theory is that England is governed by King, Lords and Commons : but it is not so in fact. The monarch does not govern ; the House of Lords is not possessed of equal authority with the Hous of Commons "—that is what Bagehot sets out to show his readers, and he does it with an ease, a humour and a familiarity that are far more effective than the austere logic of Mill and Austin, or the picturesque invective of Carlyle. Indeed the vogue which *Physics and Politics* attained is largely due to style, for the book is little more than a popular and concise version of the conclusions of Sir Henry Maine and Herbert Spencer about progress. The book appeared about 1876, and I remember that as I was going in for Greats at Oxford it was put into my hands as the thing I must read. Of the charm and force of

Bagehot's style at its best the following passage is an example:

" Success in life, then, depends, as we have seen, more than anything else on 'animated moderation,' on a certain combination of energy of mind and balance of mind, hard to attain and harder to keep. And this subtle excellence is aided by all the finer graces of humanity. It is a matter of common observation that, though often separated, fine taste and fine judgment go very much together, and especially that a man with gross want of taste, though he may act sensibly and correctly for a while, is yet apt to break out, sooner or later, into gross practical error. In metaphysics, probably both taste and judgment involve what is termed ' poise of mind,' that is the power of true passiveness, the faculty of ' waiting ' till the stream of impressions whether those of life or those of art, have done all that they have to do, and cut their full type plainly upon the mind. . . . In this way the union between a subtle sense of beauty and a subtle discretion in conduct is a natural one, because it rests on the common possession of a fine power, though, in matter of fact, that union may be often disturbed . . . And therefore the cultivation of a fine taste tends to promote the function of a fine judgment, which is a main help in the complex world of civilized existence."

It was in the quality of " animated moderation " that Bagehot claimed that the English excelled all other nations—the power of going with a swing but pulling up in time—and to it he ascribed their success.

" There is an infinite deal to be laid against us, and as we are unpopular with most others, and as we are always grumbling against ourselves, there is no want of people to say it. But, after all, in a certain sense, England is a success in the world; her career has had many faults, but still it has been a fine and winning career on the whole. And this on account of the exact possession of this particular quality."

It is well to remember that *The English Constitution*, on which Bagehot's fame will chiefly rest, was written in 1864, at the height of Palmerston's power, and before Disraeli's Reform Act of 1867 was passed. In 1872 Bagehot wrote an Introduction to the second edition in which, as the result of household suffrage, a good deal of the complacent optimism of a Palmerstonian is replaced by an ultra-Tory distrust of democracy. But without a practical, personal acquaintance with the men and things of politics *The English Constitution* could not have been written. Bagehot stood three times for Parliament—for Manchester, for Bridgwater (his own country), and for the London University. He was unsuccessful in all these attempts, which is not surprising, for the philosopher is seldom popular on the platform, and his biographer tells us that he had no power of speaking in public. I cannot imagine Walter Bagehot trapesing through the lobbies at the bidding of the Whips, or sitting for days and weeks behind the Treasury bench with an undelivered speech on the Budget in his hand. But like Thackeray and Trollope he utilized his electoral experiences for his book. The two best elections in fiction are those in *The Newcomes* and in *Ralph the Heir;* and much of the humorous realism in *The English Constitution* was obviously based on personal contact with the " free and independent " electors of Taunton. Bagehot handles the component parts of the English Constitution analytically. He takes the Monarchy, the House of Lords, and the House of Commons, and he asks of each the searching, awkward, modern question, of what use is this thing ?

" The use of the Queen," he writes, " in a dignified capacity, is incalculable. Without her in England, the present English Government would fail and pass away. Most people when they read that the Queen walked on the slopes of Windsor—that the Prince of Wales went to the Derby—have imagined that too much thought and prominence were given to little things. But they have been in error ; and it is nice to trace how the actions of a retired widow and an unemployed youth become of such importance."

Supposing this to have been true of Queen Victoria and her son (the late King), is it true any longer ? Remember that Bagehot wrote before Mr. Forster's first Education Act, long before primary education had been made (by the Tories) not only compulsory, but gratuitous. What do the generation trained in the County Council schools think of kingship ? Bagehot says, truly enough, that Monarchy is intelligible, whereas democracy (i.e. without Monarchy) is a government of difficult ideas. But when we are told that the vast majority of people regard the Sovereign as God's anointed, and as really the government that rules their daily lives by a mystical, divine right, I doubt. The reigning family is described as the most important of the dignified and theatrical parts of the Constitution, which attracts the obedience used by statesmen to carry on the government. This was no doubt true in the Palmerstonian period; is it true to-day? Do the King and Queen and their children attract obedience, or merely the curiosity of the gossiping, foolish crowd? If the dignified and theatrical parts of the Constitution do *not* attract the obedience that is to be used by its efficient parts, i.e. the Cabinet and the departmental offices, then Bagehot has very little to say in their favour. He handles this part of his subject with characteristic freedom.

As a rational and efficient part of the Constitution he says frankly that he has little or no use for a king. For while he admits that an experienced or intelligent Sovereign might exercise a great and useful influence in politics, particularly at moments of difficulty, when an old government is being dissolved and a new government is being formed, he is careful to impress upon us that the odds are long against the occupant of the throne being a person with an intelligence even equal to the average, or endowed with the industry necessary to profit by his experience. Whilst enumerating a string of things which the Sovereign can do theoretically but cannot do practically, Bagehot regards the veto on legislation as dead, and is disposed to leave the King three means of interfering with politics—the power of dismissing a Prime Minister, the power of dissolving Parliament, and the power of creating peers.

It is certain that the King can dismiss a Prime Minister by refusing to take his advice. William IV did so in 1834, when he dismissed Lord Melbourne and called on Sir Robert Peel to form a government, which did not live five months. Bagehot observes that the power of dissolving Parliament might be in the hands of a discerning monarch a most valuable check upon the abuse of power by the Cabinet. The Sovereign, being detached from political parties, might be an impartial umpire, and might decide when an appeal might be made to the nation from a Prime Minister with a majority in the House of Commons. But Bagehot was obsessed, like Hamilton and the Federalists, by the figure of George III, whom he persistently regarded as " a meddling maniac."

He is afraid that the average king will not be able to form a good judgment on the question whether the Prime Minister is supported by the nation or not, and so will either be too timid to use his prerogative, or will use it at the wrong time. With regard to the creation of peers, it is rather striking to find that Bagehot regards " the catastrophic creation of peers," namely, the swamping process with which Mr. Asquith threatened the House of Lords in 1911, as out of the with a firm conviction that it is theft. Nobody saw more clearly than Bagehot that our system of government, with its "triple bond" of Kings, Lords, and Commons, rested on the deferential spirit of the nation, the willingness of those without property and mind to obey those who had property and mind. He agreed that the right of the House of Lords to form a part of the government could exist only so long as it was unquestioned, and that it must disappear as soon as it came to be bawled about on platforms. But it was unthinkable to Bagehot that the spirit of deference, the habit of obeying his betters, could ever be eradicated from the nature of the average Englishman.

Indeed nothing illustrates more impressively the distance we have travelled from the Palmerstonian period than the fact that Bagehot should praise the House of Lords for the attributes it has lost, and blame it for lacking those which it has recently shown itself to possess. The House of Lords is useful, according to the author of *The English Constitution,* as a dignified and dramatic part of government, as imposing on the imagination of the middle and lower classes, as saving us from the worship of wealth and office, as attracting obedience for the Cabinet to use in what Johnson called "driving on the system of things." The House of Lords is not useful, is blameworthy, as a chamber to revise the bills of the House of Commons, because the majority of peers know nothing about business and do not take the trouble to attend.

"The Corn Laws are gone: the pocket boroughs are gone: why tease about clause 6 in a railway bill?" Such is Bagehot's humorous description of the state of mind of the feeble and forlorn peers in the mid-Victorian era. But all this has been reversed. The peers have ceased to attract obedience by their dignity or show; they have not saved us from the thrall of the millionaire and the Government official. On the other hand, the House of Lords has become a most efficient chamber of revision for the hasty and corrupt legislation of the House of Commons. In 1910 Sir Edward Grey carried through the House of Commons the Naval Prize Bill, which gave legislative force to the Declaration of London, 1908, settled at the Hague Conference. Shortly, the Bill would have deprived England of the power of blockade by stopping neutral ships and would certainly have lost us the war. Happily on the motion of Lord Desborough it was rejected by the House of Lords.

Working as it does in the fetters of the Parliament Act, the House of Lords is now the only place where independent and first-rate discussion of politics is possible; the peers are the only check left on the absolutism of the Cabinet. But that is owing to changes in the House of Commons which Bagehot could not foresee. Disregarding the theories of the books, Bagehot describes the House of Commons as an Electoral College, whose first and most important function is that of choosing and maintaining a government. The electoral colleges in the United States are a farce, because the electors are chosen on a ticket, i.e. they are chosen to choose A or B as President, and once having dropped their ticket in the urn, their function is discharged and they are dissolved. The House of Commons, according to Bagehot, is a body of independent electors, who not only choose our Government but support it. The proper answer of a Prime Minister to criticisms on the House of Commons is "It has chosen me, and kept me in power." This original view of the chief function of the House of Commons illustrates Bagehot's curious leaning towards Cæsarism.

The legislative function of the House of Commons Bagehot almost ignores; no doubt because he knew that the Cabinet and the Treasury counsel are the real legislators. But he lays great stress upon what he calls the lyrical function of the House of Commons, and upon its informative and educational functions. The mind of the British nation upon subjects of first-rate political importance is to be expressed in the best form by the House of Commons, and a body of electors, keenly interested in politics, are to be educated by free and animated debates. If we are to have government by discussion, says one of the orators in Thucydides, let it be the best possible discussion. In truth, the highest function of a popular assembly is independent and competent criticism of the Government and of the events of the world.

The House of Lords, even with its power reduced to a suspensory veto of two and a half or at most three years, is the only place where the free and educated discussion of the measures of Government can be looked for. It might be thought that the Press would take the place of the House of Commons as an arena of argument; but the Press is in the hands of three or four men, who have made their fortunes and obtained their peerages by supporting one party or the other. Turn where we will, we are confronted by the same contempt for individual liberty, the same corrupt irrationality, the same vulgar violence. Bagehot, writing in the 'sixties, more than half a century ago, could not imagine this rapid breakdown of Cabinet Government; but that he had some misgiving as to the results of the extension of the franchise in 1867 is evident from the Introduction to the second edition of *The English Constitution* which he wrote in 1872, a few years before his death.

In the Introduction Bagehot compared presidential with parliamentary government; but here his argument is again deprived of much of its value by time, for he wrote shortly after the assassination of Lincoln and just when France was beginning the experiment after Sudan. Presidential government, in the sense of a president governing who is not responsible to the legislature, as in the United States, has little interest for us, for it is safe to predict that, whatever blunders and excesses our democracy may commit, it will not imitate the Americans in separating the executive from the legislative chambers. But presidential government as it exists in France, that is to say, the

Cabinet system with a president instead of a monarch, is within the range of possibility for Great Britain. The result in France has been that the Government is changed at least once a year on an average.

Responsible government without a Sovereign has ended in apparently incorrigible instability. Another point discussed at some length is the treaty-making power. Bagehot was struck by the absurdity of the Government, in the person of the Secretary of State for Foreign Affairs, signing treaties and agreements with foreign Powers, and then " laying papers " before Parliament for discussion. What is the use of discussion after the treaty is signed ? This question has been answered recently by the adoption of Bagehot's suggestion that a treaty should be " laid " before the House of Commons for a short time before signature. Every treaty is made subject to ratification by the House of Commons. Indeed most treaties require an Act of Parliament to implement its provisions. When the Government has no majority or a small one, this gives the House of Commons a real control over the treaty-making power of the Crown as advised by the Ministry. In 1924 Mr. Ramsay MacDonald's treaty with the Russian Soviets was not ratified, and the Labour Government, having no majority of its own, fell.

The most instructive passages in *The English Constitution* are Bagehot's reflections on Disraeli's democratic adventure. To us nowadays the Act of 1867, which abolished the rental qualification in the towns and substituted the occupation of a rateable tenement, does not seem alarming; and it was followed in 1884 by a similar reduction of the franchise in the counties. Of the fifty-nine years which have run since Disraeli's leap in the dark, the Conservatives or Unionists have been in power for twenty-three years, which would seem to justify Lord Beaconsfield. But, as Bagehot points out, the effect of laws altering the franchise depends on the spirit of those who work them, and thus the real result is nearly always delayed and concealed for at least a generation.

What is called the great Reform Bill of 1832 had no perceptible effect for more than thirty years after its passage, because it was worked by Lord Melbourne, Lord John Russell, Lord Derby, Lord Palmerston, and Sir Robert Peel, the statesmen of the pre-Reform era. Peel died in 1851; Palmerston and Derby died in 1865 and 1868; Lord Russell retired about the same time; and thus a whole generation of statesmen disappeared, and a new generation of statesmen, headed by Gladstone and Disraeli, appeared. Bagehot did not trust either of these statesmen: Gladstone, because he was too earnest and impulsive and subtle—he lacked " animated moderation "; Disraeli, because he was merely an eloquent sceptic.

Still less did he trust the new generation of electors, and believing that it is men not measures that matter, he addressed a very impressive warning to his contemporaries. As a theoretical writer he could venture to say what no elected member of Parliament, Conservative or Liberal, could venture to say, " I am exceedingly afraid of the ignorant multitude of the new constituencies." If Bagehot wrote that in 1872, what would he say in 1927 when by the Reform Act of 1918, carried through Parliament in the last agony of the war by two Conservative politicians, Speaker Lowther and Walter Long, eleven million electors have been added to the register, including women and paupers, after a few days' perfunctory debate ? This is what he did say of the policy of dishing the Whigs :

" The leading statesmen in a free country have great momentary power. They settle the conversation of mankind. It is they who, by a great speech or two, determine what shall be said and what shall be written for long after. They, in conjunction with their counsellors, settle the programme of their party—the ' Platform ' as the Americans call it, on which they, and those associated with them, are to take their stand for the political campaign. It is by that programme, by a comparison of the programmes of different statesmen, that the world forms its judgement.

"The common ordinary mind is quite unfit to fix for itself what political question it shall attend to ; it is as much as it can do to judge decently of the questions which drift down to it, and are brought before it ; it almost never settles its topics ; it can only decide upon the issues of those topics. And in settling what these questions shall be, statesmen have now especially a great responsibility. If they raise questions which will excite the lower orders of mankind ; if they raise questions on which those orders are likely to be wrong ; if they raise questions on which the interest of those orders is not identical with, or is antagonistic to, the whole interest of the State, they will have done the greatest harm they can do.

"The future of this country depends on the happy working of a delicate experiment, and they will have done all they could to vitiate that experiment. Just when it is desirable that ignorant men, new to politics, should have good issues, and only good issues, put before them, these statesmen will have suggested bad issues.

"They will have suggested topics which will bind the poor as a class together ; topics which will excite them against the rich ; topics the discussion of which in the only form in which that discussion reaches their ear will be to make them think that some new law can make them comfortable—that it is the present law which makes them uncomfortable—that Government has at its disposal an inexhaustible fund out of which it can give to those who now want without also creating elsewhere other and greater wants. If the first work of the poor voters is to try to create a 'poor man's Paradise,' as poor men are apt to fancy that Paradise, and as they are apt to think they can create it, the great political trial now beginning will simply fail. The wide gift of the elective franchise will be a great calamity to the whole nation, and to those who gain it as great a calamity as to any."

These words were written fifty-four years ago; and to Mr. Lloyd George and Mr. Ramsay MacDonald they will probably sound like " a tale told by an idiot." Nevertheless they are true; and they were never nearer to proof than at this hour.

Anthony Trollope

ANTHONY TROLLOPE
National Portrait Gallery

LIBRARY
FLORIDA STATE UNIVERSITY
TALLAHASSEE, FLORIDA

ANTHONY TROLLOPE

It says little for the taste of the last quarter of the Victorian age that Anthony Trollope's autobiography, published in 1883 by his son Henry, should have been for many years ignored or derided. A publisher, more foolish than most, exclaimed that the autobiography had killed the remnant of Trollope's reputation.

It is now recognised that the little book is the best literary life of the nineteenth century, if we except Trevelyan's Macaulay. It has the candour of Pepys, without his diffuseness and indecent familiarity. It has the brevity of Gibbon, without the stateliness of the great historian. Trollope was no hero to himself. He doesn't bore you with his pedigree or the cradle of his race, as so many men of good family, when they sit down to write their story, are prone to do. He tells you that the two objects of his life were to be Anthony Trollope—" *digito monstrari et dicier : Hic est* "—and to make enough money to enjoy himself and provide for his family.

> " It will not, I trust, be supposed that I have intended in this so-called autobiography to give a record of my inner life. No man ever did so truly— and no man ever will. If the rustle of a woman's petticoat has ever stirred my blood ; if a cup of wine has been a joy to me ; if I have thought tobacco at midnight in pleasant company to be one of the elements of an earthly paradise ; if now and

again I have somewhat recklessly fluttered a five pound note over a card-table—of what matter is that to any reader? I have betrayed no woman. Wine has brought me to no sorrow. It has been the companionship of smoking that I have loved, rather than the habit. I have never desired to win money, and I have lost none. To enjoy the excitement of pleasure, but to be free from its vice and ill-effects—to have the sweet and leave the bitter untasted—that has been my study. The preachers tell us that this is impossible. It seems to me that hitherto I have succeeded fairly well. I will not say that I have never scorched a finger—but I carry no ugly wounds."

Trollope never made any pretence of religion, and to his nature mysticism was impossible. But if there be a better defence of the apolaustic life I do not know it.

What offended or made people laugh in the autobiography was the revelation of the great novelist's methods of writing. Awakened by his groom, Trollope sat down to his desk every morning at 5 (or was it 4.30?) and, with his watch before him, wrote 250 words per fifteen minutes for three hours, when he breakfasted, and either rode on an indifferent hunter to the nearest meet or set about his duty as a Post Office inspector. He had a pad or block on which he wrote in crowded railway carriages, and a desk fixed up in his cabin when he was at sea.

It is impossible not to smile when he tells us that as he was writing that charming story of love and fox-hunting in *Framley Parsonage* he had frequently to leave a chapter unfinished on the saloon table and retire to his cabin to be sick. But if we laugh we must also admire the triumph of mind over matter. Only the ignorant could be disturbed by the steady tale of bricks in the small hours of the morning.

The ways of every art are tedious. Do we know how many times Millais or Sargent painted out the arm of a beauty? Or how many hours Tennyson or Swinburne spent over their stanzas? Trollope, a little perversely, pours scorn on the inspiration of art, and insists a trifle too much that the making of books is a trade, like the making of any other article in which success is only and always attainable by steady and punctual industry.

In the course of thirty years, between 1853 and his death in 1882, Trollope published some fifty books, of which forty-seven were novels, nearly all in three volumes, and he made about £75,000. One habit he had which he shared with Henry James. The morning after he had finished a novel he began another. He boasts of having written more than Carlyle and as much as Voltaire. To have been the most prolific writer of his day and at the same time an efficient servant of the Post Office is something of which a man in his closing years may fairly be proud.

The Warden was the first of the Barsetshire series and the foundation of Trollope's fortune, though at the time of its publication, and for three years after, he received from his publisher £19. In later years he derived a comfortable income from it as one of the group. " In the course of the job I visited Salisbury, and whilst wandering there one midsummer evening round the purlieus of the Cathedral, I conceived the story of *The Warden*." A wag, who was himself a high official in the Post Office, explained Trollope's extraordinary insight into the life of the Close and clerical character by declaring that the inspector opened the letters of the Bishop and Dean and Chapter.

Trollope, who would have died rather than own an imagination, assures us that he evolved the Barchester dignitaries out of his " moral consciousness." He drew what he thought an archdeacon should or would be, and Archdeacon Grantly stood out, clear-cut and lifelike. The Bishop and Mrs. Proudie are perhaps the highest reach of Trollope's protraiture in the clerical line. The great masters of characterisation—Thackeray, Balzac, Carlyle, Macaulay—took pains to get their scenery right. Carlyle visited Germany, and Macaulay Ireland and the Midlands, with this object. Trollope took no such trouble, and though he learned the ritual life of the Cathedral, and discoursed about precentors and rural deans correctly enough, he got into a mess when he took to describing lawyers and politicians.

Whatever he wrote about the Civil Service—in Sir Raffle Buffles he got back a bit of his own on Maberly and Rowland Hill—or about fox-hunting, was first-hand knowledge. But he knew less about the procedure of the law than most laymen, certainly less than the son of a barrister ought to know. No novelist or dramatist need introduce a trial at bar; but if he does, he should get it right, or he spoils his effect. The trial of Lady Mason in *Orley Farm* is a tissue of absurdities and blunders, which Sir Francis Newbolt has ruthlessly exposed. Nevertheless, the character of Furnival, the elderly and eloquent common law counsel, who is brought down " special," though he is only a " stuff," to defend Lady Mason, with whom he is in love, is well done, that is to say, as to his senile philandering and his crossness to his wife. Chaffenbrass, too, is a good caricature of the Old Bailey barrister as he was, though he does have chambers in Ely-place! In the whole range of his novels Trollope is only really successful with one lawyer, both as to character and to setting.

It is a striking instance of how an author may misjudge his works that Trollope should declare *Ralph the Heir* to be the worst of his novels, and to have clean forgotten Sir Thomas Underwood, ex-solicitor general and defeated candidate for Percy-cross. Unhesitatingly I give my opinion that *Ralph the Heir* is one of the best of the novels, and that Sir Thomas Underwood, as a retired leader of the Bar, excusing his idleness by a *magnum opus* on Francis Bacon, of which he never wrote a line, is one of the greatest creations in fiction.

Trollope's politics are sad trash, though again, as with lawyers, the characterisation of the minor persons is masterly. What sticks are Mr. Gresham (Gladstone) and Mr. Daubigny (Disraeli)! Was there ever a more futile and impossible hero than Phineas Finn? A penniless Irish adventurer, who says little or nothing, but who, his creator tells us, is good-looking and pleasant, especially to women, is easily promoted to Ministerial rank and married to a wealthy and fashionable widow, when all the time there is no reason for his existence. All our novelists have tried their hand at the English gentleman, and all have failed. Fielding's Allworthy is too good; Dickens has given us Sir Leicester Dedlock, a purely fanciful sketch. Colonel Newcome, for all his Don Quixote manners, carries his foolishness in money matters to the point of criminality. Mr. Brooke of Tipton is a rambling old boy whose discursiveness and indolence allow Dorothea to marry Casaubon.

Trollope tells us that if Plantagenet Palliser, Duke of Omnium, was not a great English gentleman, then he knew not the meaning of the term. Planty Pal as a member of society is a prig: as a politician he is a poop; as husband and father he is pompous and unsympathetic. All my sympathy is with Lady Glencora, whom Trollope puts down as vulgar, but whom I love, if her manners do give a little in the heroine of musical comedy. Trollope comes, unconsciously, much nearer to the mark in Squire Dale, who keeps up an old place on a straitened income, or in Lord de Guest, in *The Small House at Allington*. *The Claverings* and *The Way we Live Now*, are great novels, but little known.

Apart from his characterisation, Trollope had a few fixed simple ideas about young men and women, which run through all his novels. He thought it not only excusable, but normal that a young man should be in love with two and sometimes three young women at the same time. Phineas Finn, after he had buried his Irish wife, was in love with Lady Laura Kennedy, Lady Chiltern, and Madame Max Gœsler, if not quite simultaneously very soon after one another. Harry Clavering is angrily in love with Julia Brabazon, who married Lord Ongar, and hardly had the church bells stopped, when he engages himself to plain Florence Burton. On the return from abroad of Lady Ongar, a rich and beautiful widow, now able to avow her love for Harry, the young fool wobbles for some time in Trollopian fashion, and finally sticks to Florence, whose brother, the architect, wipes his shoes with his handkerchief. Ralph Newton makes love to one cousin, proposes to another, is engaged to his tailor's daughter, and finally marries or is married by the daughter of a neighbouring squire. Trollope's commonsense realism taught him that the tearing, raging passion of which poets sing and novelists write is the creation of their fancy and has no existence in human nature. Love in young men he knew well enough was a transient, tepid, and if intense, then quickly changing emotion. But this fluency of feeling which he generously allowed to his young men, he forbade to his young women, who were all of the constant, clinging, quiet, much enduring type, short, brown-haired and brown-eyed in appearance, like Florence Burton, Lucy Morris, Grace Crawley and Lucy Robarts. Constancy is, indeed, carried so far in Lily Dale as to amount to obstinacy, and many of his readers begged Trollope to allow the manly virtues of John Eames to be rewarded. But the slaughter of Mrs. Proudie was the utmost concession he would make to popular clamour. On girls who sold themselves for money or a title he had no mercy, and the punishment allotted to Lady Clavering, Julia Ongar, and Laura Kennedy has always seemed to me to be too severe. Of all his young women, Mary Thorne is the most attractive.

Though Trollope called himself a Liberal, and under that label once contested the borough of Beverley, the following passage from " Doctor Thorne " discovers an attitude towards the landed aristocracy which to-day would be derided as antediluvian Toryism.

Writing of the Greshams of Greshamsbury, he says, " But the old symbols remained, and may such symbols long remain among us ; they are still lovely and fit to be loved. They tell us of the true and manly feelings of other times ; and to him who can read aright, they explain more fully, more truly than any written history can do, how Englishmen have become what they are. England is not yet a commercial country in the sense in which that epithet is used for her ; and let us hope that she will not soon become so. She might surely as well be called feudal England or chivalrous England. If in Western civilised Europe

there does still exist a nation among whom there are
high signors, and with whom the owners of the land
are the true aristocracy, the aristocracy that is trusted
as being the best and fittest to rule, that nation is the
English. Choose out the ten leading men of each
great European people. Choose them in France, in
Austria, Sardinia, Prussia, Russia, Sweden, Denmark,
Spain, and then select the ten in England whose names
are best known as those of leading statesmen; the
result will show in which country there still exists the
closest attachment to, the sincerest trust in, the old
feudal and now so-called landed interests." This
passage reads romantically to-day, and yet it was
written in my infancy by the most Victorian of
novelists. Trollope's appreciation of the clerical
aristocracy was no less hearty.

" The dean was one of those old-world politicians—
we meet them every day, and they are generally
pleasant people—who enjoy the politics of the side
to which they belong without any special belief in
them. If pressed hard they will almost own that their
so-called convictions are prejudices. But not for
worlds would they be rid of them. When two or three
of them meet together, they are as freemasons, who
are bound by a pleasant bond which separates them
from the outer world. They feel among themselves
that everything that is being done is bad—even though
that everything is done by their own party. . . Education Bills and Irish Land Bills were all bad. Every
step taken has been bad. And yet to them old England

is of all countries in the world the best to live in, and is not at all the less comfortable because of the changes that have been made. These people are ready to grumble at every boon conferred on them, and yet to enjoy every boon. They know, too, their privileges, and, after a fashion, understand their position. It is picturesque, and it pleases them. To have been always in the right and yet always on the losing side; always being ruined, always under persecution from a wild spirit of republican demagogism—and yet never to lose anything, not even position or public esteem, is pleasant enough. A huge, living, daily increasing grievance that does one no palpable harm, is the happiest possession that a man can have. There is a large body of such men in England, and personally they are the very salt of the nation. He who said that all Conservatives were stupid did not know them. Stupid Conservatives there may be—and there certainly are very stupid Radicals. The well-educated, widely-read Conservative, who is well assured that all good things are gradually being brought to an end by the voice of the people, is generally the pleasantest man to be met."

There is truth as well as humour in this portrait of the upper middle-class Conservative, drawn as it was more than half a century ago. Yet how far off it seems, like a page from the eighteenth century! This too was part of the Victorian tradition.

… Benjamin Jowett

BENJAMIN JOWETT

THESE sketches of men of light and leading in the last quarter of Queen Victoria's reign call for a glance at the Great Oxford Head who moulded the early mind of so many of them. The Master of Balliol was the guide, philosopher and friend of Sir Robert Morier and Lord Lansdowne, of Lords Oxford, Milner, and Curzon, and of a great many able editors, whose lot is to bear the cross of anonymity. Jowett's influence therefore was pervasive, and extended unperceived beyond the walls of that hideous building, a cross between a barrack, a workhouse, and a modern convent, which covers nearly the whole of one side of the Broad, almost smothering graceful little Trinity.

When I went up in 1874 the intellectual primacy of Balliol was unquestioned and indisputable. It was in a class by itself. After it came four reading colleges of much distinction, Corpus, University, New College, and St. John's. Christ Church, since the spacious times of Harry Chaplin and Walter Long were past, was still mourning the abolition of gentlemen commoners with their yellow tassels, and withdrew in haughty seclusion from the common current of University life.

" The House " turned its back on the river, and absolutely ignored the Union. Cricket it did play and cards, but in the seclusion of Bullingdon.

In my day Christ Church was in its transition

period, and was neither fowl, nor flesh, nor good red herring. It did not mix with and lead "the young barbarians all at play," like Brasenose and Magdalen; it had ceased to be high-born, and was not yet high or even mezzo-brow. All this is changed now, for I remember that in last year's (1926) Eight Christ Church contributed nearly half the crew. But at the time of which I am speaking the Cardinal's hat on a blazer was seldom seen in the streets,—men wore blazers, not bags, and also cap and gown untorn in the High—and I cannot remember anyone at The House in the seventies who did anything in after life except Lord Newton. The eclipse of Cardinal Wolsey's glorious abbey, which ought always to be the first college in Oxford, was the work of Jowett, who had routed the stately Liddell in the fight for the sons of the great families.

Balliol had gutted The House, and the Master, with his squeaky voice and round face, and cold commemorative eye, had stolen the gilded youth from the Dean. Perhaps too, the upper classes were beginning to realize—they have a wonderful gift of intelligent anticipation—that the world was changing for their sons, who might conceivably be called upon at some more or less distant date to compete with intellectuals, " not bred in our kennel," to repeat the coarse phrase which a Whig peer applied to Gladstone. The Russells, Leveson-Gowers, Charterises, Fitzmaurices, Wallops, Portals, who would automatically have proceeded, in the previous generation, from Eton to Christ Church, now matriculated at Balliol, and were told they must read for honours.

The test of a great speech is whether it produces a change in the position of the speaker, as mirrored in the opinion of those around him. In 1877 I made a speech at the Union against Gladstone's Bulgarian atrocities agitation which transformed me in a night from nobody to somebody in my college and the University. I was elected President of the Union without opposition at the beginning of the next term. Balliol dons and scholars, who had looked askance at the commoner in loud checks and an eyeglass, now hailed me with "nods and becks and wreathed smiles." On Jowett the effect of the speech was magical.

The Master had sent me down the term before for some tipsy revel, with expressions of cold contempt. He now invited me to spend a part of the next Long at his Malvern villa, an honour rarely extended to any but scholars and exhibitioners. That was Jowett. As a host nobody could have been more charming, though his sherry was rather fiery, not to be allayed by his piping assurance that it was Amontillado. Dear old man! He used to walk me round the Beacon, dropping into my ear maxims about life and comments on its actors. The result was cumulative and remembered long afterwards. Two of his sayings only remain familiar, but wise enough, repeated probably to scores of his young friends, " never disappoint people," and " never explain yourself." I can't say I have observed either.

Jowett was fond of saying that Boswell was a genius, and some of his friends and pupils interpreted this judgment into a half-conscious wish that he, too, had been lucky enough to find a patient worshipper always at his elbow to record his conversation. Dr. Evelyn Abbott and Dr. Lewis Campbell have done much, both by their previous *Life* and by the later volume of *Letters*, to give the world a nearer view of the greatest college Head of his day. But neither *Life* nor *Letters* can give any idea of Jowett's daily talk, which was quite as remarkable in its way as that of Dr. Johnson.

Jowett and Johnson had truly many striking points of difference, but they were superficial, or related to those habits which are the result of circumstances rather than an expression of character. Dr. Johnson was a slovenly Bohemian, idle, and often intemperate. Dr. Jowett detested Bohemianism and eccentricity of all kinds, was a model of neatness in his dress, and a pattern of precision in his hours. Johnson bawled and Jowett chirped; but the mental attitude of the two men towards the world and their fellow-creatures was the same. Both had the virtue, or the vice, of incredulity, and the Master of Balliol hesitated as little as the Sage of Fleet Street to give the lie direct to anyone whom he disbelieved.

The pendant to Johnson's " Sir, don't tell that story again : you can't think how poor a figure you make in telling it," was Jowett's favourite comment, " There's a great deal of hard lying in the world, especially amongst people whose character it is impossible to suspect." Both moralists had a hearty contempt for the *cui bono* school of philosophy, and perhaps an exaggerated admiration for those who, in Johnson's words, are helping to drive on the system of the world. In the presence of both, intellectual pretension stood abashed, and loose talk was repressed. Both practised conversation not merely as an art but as a duty, and both influenced their generation a great deal more by their spoken than their written words.

We doubt, for instance, whether any one ever rose a stronger or a wiser man from reading a number of the *Rambler* or a page of *Rasselas*; but we are quite sure that no one left Dr. Johnson's company without feeling that his moral constitution had been braced up. Dr. Jowett's translations of Plato and Thucydides are models of what a crib should be, for they manage to preserve the spirit of Greek and the style of English. But though their public may be increased by the spread of middle-class education, it is not on those works that the fame of their author rested or ever will rest. Jowett's influence was derived from his talk, at his own table, in his study, in the Balliol quadrangle, in his rambles round the Malvern Hills, with undergraduates, and with men of the world.

He had as shrewd an eye for an undergraduate as a Yorkshireman has for a horse, and he spotted his Milners, his Asquiths, and his Curzons, with the certainty born of practice. If he trained his winners with more assiduity than his crocks, who shall blame him?

Not that he could not be very kind to some of his shabbier pupils, but he was not so to all, and on industrious mediocrity he refused to waste his time. Jowett was often accused of " tuft-hunting,"of paying more attention to undergraduates of social position than to the Browns, Joneses, and Robinsons, and of preferring the company of the great one of the earth. This was not due to snobbishness, but to his intuitive grasp of the realities of life, for, as he once said in a sermon, " Rank is not a dispensation of Providence, but it is a fact." There was another, and quite harmless, explanation of his undoubted preference for those whose manners were easy.

When he began his career at the Master's Lodge, Jowett was unaccustomed to society, and a little ill at ease ; indeed, he never quite lost his shyness. He therefore liked people who were not afraid of him, fashionable women who rattled, undergraduates who " cheeked " him in the well-bred, Etonian way. To intellectual fear he was a stranger ; and he would tackle Lord Salisbury, Mr. Gladstone, or Matt. Arnold with equal intrepidity.

What was the secret of his personal influence ? As in the case of Johnson, Jowett's conversation (in which we include his letters) drew its power from an extraordinary, and apparently intuitive, insight into human life and character. There is no more wonderful faculty possessed by genius of a certain kind than that of seeing into and through phases of life of which it can have no experience.

Anthony Trollope, when he wrote *Barchester Towers*, was a Post Office inspector, who had never set foot, except casually, in a cathedral close. The advice Johnson gave to Boswell about practising at the bar might have come from the oldest bencher in the Temple. Jowett had this gift of worldly intuition in a remarkable degree, and the science of life was with him a passion. When therefore he gave counsel to one of his favourite pupils or to an intimate friend, the hearer was immediately struck by its incisive shrewdness. This quality of worldly wisdom comes out very strongly in his letters to Sir Robert Morier, who was one of his few close friends. Take, for example, this passage from a letter to the celebrated diplomatist :

> " If I might advise (positively for the last time) on this joyful occasion, I would urge upon you once more ' caution and reticence.' I do not mean as to keeping of secrets, and I know that there must be a give and take of information. But what you do not appear to me to see is, that you cannot speak indiscriminately against Gladstone, Harcourt and other persons, who are for the moment influential, without raising a great deal of prejudice against yourself, and creating unnecessary drawbacks in the accomplishment of objects which you have at heart. Everyone knows how another speaks of him, and cannot be expected to love his assailant. Everybody acknowledges your ability, but I believe that the persons whose opinions you most value, feel that this defect of which you never seem to be aware has nearly shipwrecked you. May I give you as a motto for a

diplomatist my favourite sentence out of Fielding:
' I forgave him, not from any magnanimity of soul, still less from Christian charity, but simply because it was expedient for me.' Or, to put the thought in a more unworldly phrase, I forgave him simply because, having the interests of England and Europe at heart, I have no room for personal enmities or antipathies."

Sounder advice was surely never addressed to a rising man with a bitter tongue. Or take this sentence from a letter to Lord Lansdowne.

" Measures of precaution are never justly appreciated, because when most effectual they are never seen to be necessary."

It is only when thought over that the profound and mellow wisdom of this saying is apparent. Or consider this passage from another letter to the same correspondent:

" I want to urge upon you that the real time for making a reputation and gaining a position in politics is when you are out of office. Then you have independence and can act for yourself, and can make a carefully prepared speech. The difference between a man who has made a remarkable speech, whether in or out of Parliament, is enormous. To do it requires not natural eloquence, but a great deal of nerve, great industry, and familiar knowledge of a subject, and feeling about it. I do really believe that for a politician no pains can be too great about speaking. An important speech should be written out two or three times, and never spoken exactly as it was written. When once a person has gained the power of saying a few words in a natural manner to a large audience, he can hardly write too much." Yet Jowett had no practical experience of diplomacy or politics.

So much has already been said and written of Jowett's sermons that one has no inclination to say much of him as a divine. Sydney Smith said he went to church because it was his trade; and though Jowett was a militant member of the Broad Church his heart was never in theological controversy. He went to church at Malvern because he was a clergyman; but when he was bored by the sermon of the local pastor, he would calmly take out a pocket-book and make notes about Plato or Thucydides, " Noscitur e sociis " is as true in religious matters as in anything else, and Hang-Theology Rogers was one of Jowett's cronies. He is quite cross with Sir Robert Morier for proposing to write a book about Dr. Döllinger and the New Catholics.

" There is no harm," he writes, " in entering a little into religious controversy. You have had great opportunities of learning, and no doubt the friendship of such a man as Döllinger is well worth having. But I would rather write about great questions of European policy or social life. The New Catholic movement is nothing, or very little, but Bismarck is a great deal, whether the time has come for him to descend from earth or not."

That is as characteristic of the man as anything in his correspondence. Great questions of European policy or social life are what he would be at; a religious movement is nothing to him. Dr. Johnson was violently agitated by the suggestion that had he gone to the bar he would have been Lord Chancellor. It may be questioned whether a keen man of the world like Jowett was happy as a college don. If it is possible to judge from letters and after-dinner talk, he was quite contented. He had the serenity which comes from clearness and balance of mind, and if he was only a spectator, he had the satisfaction of knowing that many of the leading actors had learnt their parts from him.

Mr. "Jim" Lowther

Mr. "JIM" LOWTHER

LORD BEACONSFIELD said many years ago that to be in the House of Commons without being in London Society was like playing a game of blind man's buff.

The saying is no longer as true as it was. Society, by increasing its size, has diminished its power, and it is nowadays obliged to share a lessened influence with a well-informed Press. Everyone can mention several instances of men who have worked their way to the front rank in politics without any assistance from society. But there is still a great deal of truth left in the observation, for in every popular assembly the fact of a man's being in the social swim will always confer upon him a certain prestige.

Mr. James Lowther was "in the swim," and a good deal of his peculiar influence and position in the House of Commons was due to the knowledge that he was as much at home at Newmarket and Marlborough House as at Westminster. Even those Englishmen who know as little about the pasterns of a horse as Dr. Johnson have an unbounded respect for a Steward of the Jockey Club. A wealthy bachelor, "Jim" Lowther knew everybody, heard everything, went where he liked, and said what he pleased. Yet he was never known to abuse a confidence or a friend.

And this leads me to note that, apart from the *cachet* of his position on the turf and in society, Mr.

James Lowther had moral qualities which are all too rare, but which never fail to secure their possessor the respect of his acquaintances and the affection of his friends. Mr. Lowther was as straight as a die; he was absolutely truthful; he knew no fear; he was perfectly loyal to his associates, whether in business or pleasure. But he expected other people to treat him as he treated them, and the writer remembers his complaining of the desertion of a colleague, who had promised to support him in moving some amendment or resolution. " I have seen some shabby tricks played on the turf in my day," said Mr. Lowther sadly, " but I really can't remember anything more shabby than Wharton's not turning up this afternoon."

He never forgot or dropped anybody. For a great many years Mr. Lowther used to invite some two dozen of his Parliamentary friends to an annual dinner at his house in Grosvenor Street or at the Bachelor's Club. Naturally, a good many of his original guests fell out of Parliament; but Mr. Lowther, though he added to his list, never struck off a name, and went on inviting and receiving the ex-M.P. with as much cordiality as if he was still an active and important colleague. His good breeding and self-possession never failed him in any company, and if he seldom said a witty thing, he never said a rude one.

There is a French proverb that it takes a bad heart to say a good thing, and in conversation Mr. Lowther was shrewd and sympathetic rather than brilliant. He never tried to score off anybody, knowing well the danger of the habit. He sometimes rambled a little in narrative, but his voice was so melodious and so well modulated that his listener was not fatigued. His exquisite courtesy and consideration for other people's feelings were based on something better than training—namely, on real kindness of nature. Such a man is bound to be loved. He was probably the recipient of a good many confidences, for he was just " the man of the world " whom men and women would consult in a difficulty. He was rather like Lord Eskdale in *Coningsby*, who is said to have been the Lord Lonsdale of Disraeli's youth.

In public life the position of Mr. James Lowther was unique. He had been Under-Secretary for the Colonies and Irish Secretary under Lord Beaconsfield; but no one remembers what he did in those posts; one never thought of him as an official. Jim Lowther was a personage in the country and in Parliament; but it was as a thorough-going Tory, not as a Front-Bencher, that he loomed large in the public eye.

Apart from the question of Protection, Mr. Lowther approached politics in a spirit of good-humoured indifference. For though he had a quaint habit of speaking of men of light and leading as " damned scoundrels," and generally referring to them as unconvicted felons, the abuse was purely Johnsonian, and the strange oaths and epithets were spoken so pleasantly that not even their subjects could have been offended Once Mr. Lowther was caught in this way, for coming up from Margate in the train he was drawn into conversation by a fellow-passenger, to whom he confided that " old Sarum was a poop-stick " and " Balfour was a funker " and " Joe Chamberlain was " etc., etc. The traveller was aghast at hearing his member speak of these awful persons in this strain, and the conversation found its way into some newspaper.

Mr. Lowther was quite aware that he was regarded by his countrymen as the type of narrow-minded Tory squire, and was not above occasionally playing up or down to the part. Thus, although he spoke French unusually well for an Englishman, and was a frequent visitor to Paris, in addressing his Yorkshire or Kentish farmers, he always alluded to the Frenchman as " Mounser," and if he had occasion to mention a French statesman by name he would say " Mounser Delcassy."

I recollect once crossing from Paris to London with Mr. Lowther, and from the moment we landed at Dover no Royal Prince or Prime Minister could have been treated with more signs of respect and goodwill than the member for the Isle of Thanet. Guards walked before him to his carriage with bows and smiles and when we got to Victoria some high official rushed into the Custom's House and bawled out, " Pass Mr. James Lowther's luggage through at once!" All this was of course perfectly unsolicited and unexpected attention, for there never was a simpler, a more unaffected, and a less exacting man. It was an unbought tribute of sympathy and admiration from plain Britons to a character which they thoroughly appreciate, that of an upright, open-handed, free-spoken English gentleman, who did as he would be done by, and served his country to the best of his ability.

He certainly was no orator: in fact, he was a bad speaker, for he hummed and hawed a good deal from lack of vocabulary and from a not too copious flow of ideas. He was not above employing the arts of obstruction, for he considered everything was fair in war. And few could obstruct more artistically than Mr. James Lowther, for he knew his procedure at one time almost as well as Mr. Tim Healy, and he was always so polite that he did not excite the wrath of the Chair, or even of those against whom he was manœuvring.

Probably no one was less surprised than Mr. Lowther by Mr. Chamberlain's conversion to Protection. Either he had earlier information than the world, or the wish was father to the thought, for he was always darkly prophesying the event. He was a characteristic figure, and belonged to the régime which has long since passed away.

The type has gone, but has anything better, or as good, taken its place? The modern M.P. is a very different person from Jim Lowther, more earnest possibly, better educated in the Whitehall sense of the term. But is he as representative of the majority of his countrymen? I doubt it much.

George Wyndham

GEORGE WYNDHAM

If ever a public man, starting with every conceivable advantage, missed his mark it was George Wyndham. Let young careerists, anxious to climb to "power's meridian height," study his brief course, and try to find out for themselves why he was so brilliant a failure. Drawing upon a long and varied experience, I will give them what help I can.

It is my creed that heredity and environment divide almost equally the formation of character, and consequently the career. Both heredity and environment were against George Wyndham. If relatives choose to publish biographies within a few years of death they must endure free criticism of family matters. Wyndham was at least half a Celt; his exquisite beauty, with the dark refined features, the grace of movement, and the winning smile, were half French and half Irish Celt. His mother was the granddaughter of Lord Edward Fitzgerald and Pamela, daughter of Madame de Genlis. His father was the grandson of the last Lord Egremont, who was decidedly eccentric. If pedigree goes for anything, a certain dose of instability, or impetuosity, or rebellion against the conventional, was bound to be part of George Wyndham's mental equipment.

His environment was against solid success, because

it was too favourable. He held too good cards at the beginning of the game, and played them carelessly. Down to the end of Queen Victoria's reign the glamour of fashion was potent in a *bourgeois* House of Commons. And Wyndham was in the bull's-eye of all that was aristocratic in metropolitan society. If there is one thing next to social position that an Englishman reveres, it is the sport in which the majority of them cannot share. Wyndham hunted two, often three, days a week, and shot another two. Plenty of money he always had, and it is needless to add that his entrance and promotion in politics was made as easy for him as falling off a chair. As Burke said of his enemy the Duke of Bedford, " he was rocked and dandled into a legislator." One other temptation, the strongest of all, beset this seemingly fortunate youth. He had a genuine love of literature, particularly of poetry, of Shakespeare and mediæval French poets, of what are called in critic's slang *belles lettres*. He corresponded at great length on these subjects with Wilfrid Blunt, Gatty, Chesterton, and Belloc.

Our young careerist will, I hope, have already perceived that too many interests are a hindrance rather than a help to political success. Disraeli wrote novels only when he was out of office; and he never wasted his time in correspondence with brethren of the pen, whom he despised as heartily as Byron did. Morley practically laid aside journalism and letters when he entered Parliament. There is no more jealous mistress than politics. When you are preparing a speech or

GEORGE WYNDHAM

Elliott and Fry

listening to a debate on Irish Land Purchase it does not do to be thinking of Ronsard or Plutarch.

Versatility was the undoing of George Wyndham. He had the vanity of variety. He wanted to hunt, shoot, make speeches, be a wit among politicians, and a politician among wits. Then he had two rather serious faults. In society the easiest and most naturally sympathetic of men, his public speeches were so elaborate, both in matter and manner, that they conveyed an impression of affectation. Further, he was not exactly clear-headed, as his political letters to Arthur Balfour prove. Still, if he had stuck to English politics he would have been a success; such a success, that is, as Lord Curzon or Lord Milner.

What malign chance made Mr. Balfour appoint him Chief Secretary of Ireland? What imp of destiny made him accept the post, and entangle himself with such an Under-Secretary as Sir Antony MacDonnell and such a Viceroy as Lord Dudley? The very fact of his Fitzgerald blood ought to have been taken as a disqualification. The Irish Land Purchase Act that bears his name was Wyndham's great success. Irishmen of all parties are always civil when England is offering money or credit. So for a time, a few months, Wyndham was the best Chief Secretary ever known. Why didn't he retire with his laurels? But men never can retire after a success.

Wyndham, perhaps a little intoxicated with praise from the Nationalists, was fired with the ambition of making the Northern lion lie down with the Southern lamb. Who but George Wyndham, with his chivalry and impetuosity, would have appointed as Under-Secretary an ex-Indian official, who, to do him justice described himself in a letter to the Chief Secretary of the Tories as " an Irishman, a Roman Catholic, a Liberal in politics, with strong Irish sympathies " ? Then the Chief Secretary went for a holiday, and that Puck of Irish politics, Lord Dunraven, appeared on the scene with a scheme of Devolution, with which he managed to catch Sir Antony MacDonnell and Lord Dudley.

The whole Orange pack, pressmen and members of Parliament, started off in full cry after a Home Rule Chief Secretary, who had to bear the whole responsibility. Lord Dudley probably knew little and cared less about the whole matter. It cost Lord Dunraven nothing to drop one more scheme into his waste-paper basket. But it ruined Wyndham. Concerned rather to defend than to repudiate his Under-Secretary he resigned. " Arthur " was deeply pained, but, as in the case of his Cecil cousins, who were being hounded out of Parliament by Chamberlain's janissaries, he did nothing. There can be no doubt that Wyndham felt deeply the way in which he was abandoned by his friends at this crisis.

One other transaction contributed to the bitterness of what Dr. Mackail in his Life and Letters has described as the happiest years of his life. Like the late Lord Willoughby de Broke, Wyndham threw himself heart and soul into the opposition to Mr. Asquith's infamous Parliament Act of 1911. Like that splendid sportsman and staunch Tory, Wyndham was disgusted and enraged by the cowardice and treachery of those peers who followed Lord Lansdowne in surrendering powers of which they were the trustees for the nation. One consolation he must have found in the enthusiastic and ever-growing affection of his Dover constituents whose confidence never wavered. His feverish activity on platforms as a propagandist of Tariff Reform and Imperial Unity, and his intermittent high spirits with his friends and relatives, I read as the mask of mortification. Happily, he was spared the crowning grief of the war. In June, 1913, Wyndham died suddenly in a Paris hotel, a rare but ineffectual spirit, broken by the party machine.

Lord Chief Justice Coleridge

LORD CHIEF JUSTICE COLERIDGE

Many years ago there was published a curious correspondence between Mr. Ellis Yarnall, a cultivated American citizen with pietistic leanings, and Lord Chief Justice Coleridge. The two men met one another at very rare intervals during forty years, and then only for a few days at a time. Yet they maintained a friendship on paper by writing one another long letters on politics, on literature and on religion. They set up a literary exchange, Yarnall writing to Coleridge about the books, the leading men and the politics of America, and Coleridge shipping an equivalent cargo from England.

It might be thought that Yarnall had the best of the bargain, as he was a private individual, while Coleridge was at the centre of the legal and political world on this side. But it was not so: Yarnall's letters are quite as good as Coleridge's, sometimes better, not so well-informed as to *la haute politique*, but quite as well expressed, and often showing sounder judgment of men and events.

But the fact that the friendship was maintained by the mere bond of letters for forty years—Coleridge at any rate being a very busy man—is extraordinary, for it shows unusual intellectual curiosity and an impulse to put mind to mind which is very rare, and I fear in these days of typewriters and telephones and postcards altogether obsolete.

Another remarkable thing about the letters is that they open on the American War of Secession and close on the Home Rule struggle of 1886, two phases of the same question, on which the two men maintain the same attitude after nearly half a century. Although slavery imported a sentimental issue, the real question which the Civil War of 1861-3 decided was that of the union or the separation of the American States. Jefferson Davis was the American Parnell, and, though slavery was put forward, like landlordism in Ireland, as the grievance, the real issue was Home Rule, which is the English for " State Rights." Ellis Yarnall was a sturdy Unionist in 1861 and 1886; Coleridge was a sentimental Home Ruler in 1861 and 1886. It is amusing to find the two men furbishing up their old weapons thirty-eight years later, and urging exactly the same arguments against one another.

Nearly all lawyers, however successful, murmur against their profession. I have known many great men at the Bar whom their unemployed brethren envied, and not one of them but cursed the chain which bound him to the law courts. The truth is that a barrister has to work far harder for his income than any other money-getter, and if he has other interests in life he is apt to groan.

" One great drawback," wrote Coleridge, " there is to successful life in this country, that is, in professions or politics, which I feel daily more keenly as my life grows shorter : I mean the practical impossibility of reading largely and so as to keep the mind fresh and cultivated by the thoughts of other men . . . There is nothing compensates, to a man of heart and intelligence, for the dullness and narrowness which he finds the absorbing pursuit of a profession gradually induces upon heart and brain."

There is a curious passage in one of the letters in which the Lord Chief Justice laments his indolence, his want of law, and the inefficiency with which he does his work. He candidly admits towards the close of his life that he only remained upon the Bench in order to save more money for his second wife. Lord Coleridge was not a great lawyer in the sense that Bethell, Benjamin, Bowen, Bramwell, Cairns, and Jessel were great. He was not a great advocate, like Scarlett, or Follett, or James, or Russell, or Clarke. He was not a great Lord Chief Justice, like Mansfield, or Ellenborough, or Cockburn. And yet, being a man of great intellectual distinction, Coleridge shone by comparison with the ordinary run of Attorney-generals and judges. He had a voice clear and deep, and " musical as is Apollo's lute," which he managed perfectly, never letting it drop at the end of a sentence where the emphatic words ought to come, and never shouting, but throwing into its tones inflections of sarcasm, of protest, and of pathos. This natural gift was supported by a staccato elocution, which seemed easy, but was artistic, and by a style of diction which for grace and lucidity and dignity was unrivalled on the Bench or at the Bar.

Except where the Game Laws were concerned, the Chief Justice was a scrupulously fair and patient judge, and he was always courteous to the youngest counsel, for which in the days of Cave and Day the junior Bar was grateful. Towards the end he certainly slept a good deal. Many were the volumes of reports dropped on the floor or closed with a bang, in the hope of breaking these Jovian slumbers. But when he did awake the Chief always behaved like a gentleman by blandly ignoring the fact. Mr. Justice Cave, on the other hand, also a sleeper, when he awoke was very angry with himself, and immediately fell upon counsel, especially if he happened to be a nervous " stuff."

But Coleridge was full of feminine defects of mind and character. He was inordinately vain, and he was spiteful, and stuffed with vulgar prejudices. He made the great mistake of abolishing the Chief Justice of the Common Pleas and the Lord Chief Baron, in order that he might shine in splendid isolation as Lord Chief Justice of England. He nursed a bitter hatred against the aristocracy, which was quite unworthy of him, and made him an unjust judge when any case of poaching or trespassing was tried before him.

As a politician he was narrow-minded and uncharitable to a degree that in a man of his culture is indefensible. To Lord Coleridge Disraeli was always " the foreign mountebank," the " here-we-are-again " charlatan, the adventurer who corrupted and degraded English politics, and made the Chief Justice feel " humiliated." This judgment of Lord Beaconsfield, not delivered in the excitement of an election from the platform, but written in cold blood, contrasts foolishly with the view taken by men of all parties in the present generation. Of any sense of humour Lord Coleridge was quite devoid. I remember his saying in a speech at the Palmerston Club, " You must look at Oxford as a whole, and what a whole it is !"

It was his want of humour and solemn priggishness that made him ridiculous in the Tichborne case. Ballantine or Carson would have turned the Wapping butcher inside out in half the time it took Coleridge to plough through his elaborate and ineffective cross-examination. His " Would you be surprised to hear ?" became as much a joke as " Wait and See."

But during a murder trial on the Western Circuit he made the finest Shakespearean quotation ever heard at the Bar. It was given in evidence that the wife called to her husband (the murderer), " Come upstairs and put out the light," to which the murderer replied, " I'll put out your light." In his speech to the jury as counsel for the Crown, Coleridge quoted from *Othello*:

> "Put out the light, and then—put out the light :
> If I quench thee, thou flaming minister,
> I can again thy former light restore,
> Should I repent me ; but once put out thy light,
> Thou cunning'st pattern of excelling nature,
> I know not where is that Promethean heat,
> That can thy light relume."

Was there ever an apter or more beautiful quotation ?

What were the feelings entertained by his domestic circle for Lord Coleridge I do not know: the libel action with his son-in-law in which he was involved revealed a very bitter family quarrel. Outside his family I doubt whether he was really liked by anybody. Despite the breadth of brow and the massiveness of the nose and jaw, the eyes looked askance and the general expression was sly. Coleridge wrote of Lowell that the more he knew of him the less he liked him. " Perhaps it is because he is not really genial. Perhaps he says the same thing of me."

Perhaps he did; he spoke truth if he did. The Lord Chief Justice was an iceberg, and froze the genial currents that ran round him. The fact is Coleridge mistook his profession, which he declared was "repulsive" to him. He should have taken Orders; with his voice, his person, and his principles, he would have reigned at Lambeth.

Sir Henry Fowler
(Viscount Wolverhampton)

SIR HENRY FOWLER
(VISCOUNT WOLVERHAMPTON)

FOWLER, Ritchie, and W. H. Smith were the political products of that great middle class which ruled England from the death of Lord Palmerston in 1865 to Mr. Gladstone's death at the close of the nineteenth century. Some would add Gladstone and Peel to the list, but they would be wrong, for those two statesmen were of Eton and Christ Church; they never were engaged in any trade or profession, and belonged distinctly to the upper middle class.

As for Disraeli, he was an exotic, and belonged to no class, but the very tiny one of genius. Fowler, Ritchie, and W. H. Smith were the quintessence of the Victorian middle class, and between them there was a strong family likeness in manners, appearance, and modes of thought and expression—all were intensely serious, methodical, and inclined to be pompous. But Henry Fowler was head and shoulders above the other two in point of brains; for whereas Ritchie and Smith were dull because they had neither lucidity nor humour, Fowler was never dull, because he had lucidity, though he was quite devoid of humour.

How lamentably lacking he was in this "modulating and restraining balance-wheel," as Lowell called the sense of humour, is shown by a story which his gifted daughter tells against him. They were reading to him a passage from the proofs of *The Farringdons*—one of Mrs. Thornycroft Fowler's novels—and they came upon the satirical description of a political climber and his young helpmeet. " Have they any children ? " (asks someone in the novel). " No, only politics." Sir Henry Fowler laid down the sheets and underlined the word " No." " I shouldn't say that," he exclaimed gravely to the author, " it is too conclusive. I should say, ' not yet ' " ! And Mrs. Hamilton assures us that her father could not understand why they all laughed so much ! What is to be done with such a man ?

Henry Fowler was the family solicitor to the Radical Party, and looked the part. He was an excellent adviser, for his judgment was sound, and, having been bred an attorney, he was cautious, and knew the meaning of evidence. From another point of view, Sir Henry Fowler was one of those men, numerous enough in a reserved and shy nation, whose appearance and manner convey a very wrong impression of their inner nature. Sir Henry Fowler's carriage was severe, even to the point of being tinged with clericalism. His voice was loud and harsh, and his manner was dogmatic and domineering. Outwardly he was just what the French mean when they talk of *un homme cassant*. But in reality Henry Fowler was a warm, even tender-hearted man, sympathetic, broad in his views, and tolerant of those who differed from him. He had all the *bourgeois* respect for rank, and was deferential and partial to Lord Randolph Churchill, an attitude which that young patrician civilly reciprocated. The elation which the provincial lawyer felt at being the Queen's guest at Balmoral and petted by the duchesses and maids of honour is expressed in his letters to his family with infantine frankness.

He was in partnership for a great many years with Sir Robert Perks, and they did a big solicitor's business, financing and directing large commercial schemes, with all the provincial Nonconformist interest behind them. This occupation gave Fowler a kind of training and experience that is always rare amongst politicians, even on the Liberal side, and particularly rare on both front benches, whose occupants have, with few exceptions, been immersed from their youth in Parliamentary business, which is different from every other business in this world. In a commercial age nothing is more valuable to a statesman than personal familiarity with the routine and documents of business, bills of lading and exchange, deeds, and contracts of all kinds, from building agreements to charter-parties.

Sir Henry Fowler was thus peculiarly well equipped for the post of Financial Secretary to the Treasury, which he filled in the short Gladstone Government of 1886. In Gladstone's last Administration (1892-4) he was admitted to the Cabinet as President of the Local Government Board, and in Lord Rosebery's ill-starred ministry he was for one year Secretary of State for India. This was the zenith of a long political career, which came rather late to fruition, for Sir Henry Fowler was then sixty-five, and his speech on the Indian cotton duties was his greatest achievement. It was a critical and important occasion, for the Lancashire members had been instructed by their constituents, irrespective of party, to oppose the Government. The duties of import on cotton yarns and goods had been taken off by the Indian Government in 1882, as they were no longer needed for revenue. But in 1895, owing to the fall in the rupee, it was found necessary for revenue to re-impose the import duties, accompanied by a countervailing duty of excise on Indian cotton yarns and goods.

Sir Henry James was at that time member for Bury, and he led a powerful opposition from Lancashire to the duties. The rights and wrongs of the policy do not matter now, but Sir Henry Fowler made a very eloquent speech in defence of the Indian Government. He concluded with the following words: " My right honourable friend has said that India has no representative in this House. I deny the accuracy of that allegation. The representatives of India in this House are not one or two individuals, not even the section of members who are thought to be experts on the one hand, or those men who have a profound, a deep, and a special interest in Indian affairs on the other. Every member of this House, whether elected by an English, or by a Scotch, or by an Irish constituency, is a member for India. All the interests of India, personal, political, commercial, financial, and social, are committed to the individual and collective responsibility of the House of Commons. I ask the House to discharge that gigantic trust, uninfluenced by any selfish or party feeling, but with wisdom, and justice, and generosity."

This peroration, pronounced in a deep voice and with great emphasis, produced quite an unusual effect upon a cynical audience, and actually persuaded some of the Lancashire members to vote against Sir Henry James, whose motion was defeated by nearly three to one. Every public man has " one crowded hour of glorious life," and that was Henry Fowler's hour. He lived on that speech for the rest of his life, and shortly after the accession of the Radical Party to power in 1906 he was made Lord President of the Council, and glided away into the crimson shadows of the Upper House.

Just because Henry Fowler's type of manhood is no longer popular and powerful in the national life— indeed it may be doubted if it ever was popular, for it is not very amiable in public, whatever it may be in private—just because the provincial Nonconformist man of business, with his austerity and his angularity, is no longer the pattern of our days, we are apt to overlook the sterling qualities which underlie that character. Henry Fowler was a religious, truthful, brave, honest man, and he was an industrious and highly efficient minister of State. He had no ear for music, nor eye for art: he was not a clubbable man: he was not socially graceful or entertaining, and he afforded a tempting target for the light-glancing wit of Mr. George Russell. Still England owes something to the Puritan breed, which perhaps we can hardly do without.

Sir John Gorst

SIR JOHN GORST

Sir John Gorst's career illustrates instructively the fate of a politician who cannot make himself a good party man. What measure of social or domestic happiness Sir John Gorst enjoyed I do not know, nor is it relevant. But for a man of first-rate mental calibre, his public life was an indisputable failure. Rebellion against the bonds of party was the chief, though not the only, cause of his want of success. He never obtained complete control of his temper; he was inflexible to a point which some call obstinacy, and others tenacity; and (unlike many other men) he never managed to combine his interest at the Bar with his interest in the House of Commons.

Instead of making the politician help the lawyer, and thus pursuing his advancement along parallel lines, he contrived to set the one against the other, and thus vulgarly speaking, he fell between two stools. Having emerged from the mathematical tripos as Third Wrangler, Gorst sailed for New Zealand, falling in love, like Warren Hastings, on the voyage, though, not like the pro-consul, with another man's wife.

In the Antipodes he seems to have dabbled in missionary work and journalism, returning to England in his thirtieth year, and being called to the Bar. A year after his call he got himself elected for the town of Cambridge, a most imprudent step from a professional point of view. Two years later in 1868, he lost his seat, and at Disraeli's request he gave himself to the work of organising the Tory Party in the constituencies. In 1874 he certainly proved himself an organiser of victory, for he gave Disraeli the first and last majority in his life. And here Gorst's want of worldly wisdom, or capacity for self-advancement, first showed itself. In his hour of triumph Disraeli could have denied his Chief of the Staff nothing. Gorst asked for nothing, not even a safe and comfortable seat. He stood at a bye-election in 1875 for Chatham, at that time a troublesome, expensive and uncertain constituency.

Perhaps embittered by the lack of reward, which is never got in politics except for the asking, Gorst developed into the guerilla chief who became so famous in the Gladstonian Parliament of 1880. It was well known that Gladstone was more irritated by the " hon. and learned member for Chatham " than by any other of his many opponents, which is intelligible enough ; for Gorst's speeches were not relieved by wit or eloquence, or humour, in which he was strangely deficient; they were cold and logical statements of a case.

The Fourth Party was as torn by domestic dissension as all political combinations. The late Mr. Staveley Hill told me that he once invited the Fourth Party to a dinner party. " Arthur " could not or would not come, the fear of Uncle Salisbury being ever at the back of his head. The first of the remaining trio to arrive was Sir Henry Drummond Wolff, his natural suavity overcast by the scared and hunted look which he wore in those days. In his silkiest tones he said to his host, " If Gorst and Randolph are coming, don't put me near them, as our relations are rather strained."

Next arrived Sir John Gorst, who, fixing Drummond Wolff with his eyeglass, said in his cold and caustic tone, " My dear Hill, keep me away from Wolff, as we are not on speaking terms." Last arrived Lord Randolph Churchill, who rolled his prominent eyes round the room, and clutching his host's arm whispered fiercely, " I see you've got those damned fellows Wolff and Gorst. For God's sake put me the other side of the table, as I hate the very sight of 'em." Staveley Hill, of course, laughed, and told them to sit where they liked as it was a man's dinner.

In the summer of 1885 the Fourth Party was dissolved in office, Randolph Churchill becoming Secretary of State for India, and Gorst being made Solicitor-General, a post which was worth at that time ten or twelve thousand a year. As Gorst was a poor man with a large family, it might have been supposed that he was satisfied. On the contrary, he was, if not openly indignant, certainly fretful at being excluded from the Cabinet. Lord Salisbury's first Government was turned out six months later, in February 1886, by Gladstone and the Parnellites. The first Home Rule Bill was rejected by the House of Commons in June 1886, and the general election gave Lord Salisbury a majority.

When forming his second ministry Lord Salisbury offered Sir John Gorst the Solicitor-Generalship on the understanding that he would take the first puisne judgeship that fell vacant. Most political lawyers would say that this offer was generous payment for services to the Party. But Gorst refused it with asperity, and was finally appointed Under-Secretary for India with a salary of £1,500! These are the facts, but I cannot say whether Gorst's refusal was due to perversity, or to a consciousness that he was unfitted for high legal office. He had never had any practice at the Bar: as he went into the House of Commons a year after being called, it was impossible for him to get business as a junior.

The story was current at the Bar in 1885, though I cannot vouch for its truth, that one of the Judges in the Court of Appeal exclaimed, "Mr. Solicitor, you are ignorant of the A B C of your business." This could not have been pleasant to the proud and fiery temper of Gorst, the less so because he must have known it to be true. But though he was not what is called a tradesman-lawyer, Gorst would probably have made a good judge; certainly some of his contemporaries who were promoted to the bench knew quite as little law as he.

It was as Under-Secretary for India that I first came into contact with Sir John Gorst in the Parliament of 1886, and the occasion was interesting, as illustrating the extraordinary change of public opinion on a certain subject. The Cantonment Acts, i.e., the

C.D. Acts for India, required the sanction of Parliament, and Mr. Walter McLaren had put down a motion to repeal, or not to continue, the regulations for venereal disease. I asked Gorst in the Lobby what the Government were going to do, and he told me (very crossly) that they dared not oppose McLaren's motion! I asked whether if I, as a private member, opposed McLaren, and moved the continuance of the Acts, he would lend me the Government whips, and he very earnestly and kindly begged me not to injure my prospects by appearing as the champion of vice.

Thus was it proposed to sacrifice the health of our troops in India to Parliamentary hypocrisy, and I have lived to read the Report of the Royal Commission on Venereal Diseases!* Gorst afterwards became Financial Secretary to the Treasury, and then Vice-President of the Education Committee. He was always in hot water, and always quarrelling with his chiefs. He was offered the post of High Commissioner of South Africa, and refused it, because he would not abandon his ambition of entering the Cabinet.

Gorst cordially disliked Chamberlain and distrusted his methods. As Chamberlain was rapidly dominating the Tory Party, Gorst threw up his office in 1902, and opposed the Protectionist propaganda. Of course, he lost his seat at Cambridge University in 1905, and then his genuine, if somewhat morbid, sympathy with the suffering of poverty, the fruit of his deep religious

---

*I believe the Government of India managed to evade or ignore the House of Commons vote.

feelings, expressed itself in political socialism. He stood as a Radical in 1910 for his native town of Preston, and was beaten. His brother dying shortly afterwards, he succeeded to his estate, and ended his life as a Wiltshire squire. Sir John Gorst was a brave, conscientious, public-spirited man, with a first-class brain; but his disposition was froward, and was the main obstacle to his worldly success.

Sir Michael Hicks-Beach
(Earl of St. Aldwyn)

SIR MICHAEL HICKS-BEACH
(EARL OF ST. ALDWYN)

Sir Michael Hicks-Beach filled many of the highest positions in the State : Secretary of State for the Colonies, Chief Secretary to the Lord Lieutenant, Chancellor of the Exchequer, and President of the Board of Trade. He was one of the best administrators of the Victorian period, in the sense that he made very few mistakes and seldom got into scrapes. But he will not stand out as a distinct figure in history, as he had no creative or original power, and no definite or brilliant achievement can be placed to his credit.

He was, in short, a statesman of the clear-headed, strong-willed, industrious type, who eschews sonorous generalities, and sticks close to the business in hand. His parliamentary speaking was of a very high order ; clear, incisive, correct, no repetitions, no stumbling over his transitions with a " Well, Sir," or " Now, Sir." That made his budget speeches easier to listen to than any I ever heard, not excepting Gladstone's, and he wisely never attempted the higher flights of oratory.

The triumph of the confectioner's art is the *soufflée de surprise*, a hot pudding embosomed in a coating of ice. Sir Michael Hicks-Beach was a *soufflée de surprise*. The inside of him was as hot as ginger in the mouth : the outside of him in the House of Commons was like an iceberg, sailing amid the cross-currents of party. He was the only Minister I ever knew with whom it was better to deal on the floor of the House than in his private room.

As President of the Board of Trade in '88 or '89 he was conducting an electric lighting Bill through the Commons. I had put down an amendment for Committee, but having been told by Lord Salisbury that, before opposing a Minister in public, a political supporter should first exhaust the resources of private conference, I betook myself to the great man's room behind the Speaker's Chair to talk over my amendment. To my astonishment, I was greeted with a volley of oaths—good, round, mouth-filling oaths—such as I had not heard since I left Wellington. Mortally offended by this roughness, I moved my amendment an hour or two later, when, to my still greater astonishment, the President of the Board of Trade, in his silkiest tones, accepted the amendment of his honourable friend, almost gratefully!

It is fair to add that I received the same evening a letter from Sir Michael apologising for the warmth of his language in his private room. I never afterwards attempted to do any business with him except on the floor of the House.

Hicks-Beach's clearness of vision and soundness of judgment amounted almost to genius, and made him a very valuable counsellor, though he was not fitted to lead. When Mr. Gladstone was turned out on the beer duty in July, 1885, Sir Michael Hicks-Beach became Chancellor of the Exchequer, and Leader of the House of Commons, while Lord Randolph Churchill became Secretary of State for India.

The General Election which followed in the autumn left the two English parties equal, with Parnell holding the balance with his eighty Nationalists. Whether Lord Salisbury saw his way to a deal with Parnell or with Gladstone I do not know; but he met Parliament in January 1886. An amendment to the Address on the subject of the Burmese War was moved, and Lord Randolph Churchill, as Secretary of State for India, was sitting with his official box on his knees, listening to Gladstone, who had intervened with a history, financial and military, of all Burmese wars. Suddenly Randolph drew a paper from the box, and, clutching Beach's arm, said excitedly : " I have the old man on toast. Shall I give it him now, or shall I keep it for my Indian Budget ?" Beach answered coolly : " Give it him now. You may never introduce your Indian Budget." Accordingly, Lord Randolph followed, and with many dates and figures (supplied from the paper from the box), and much playful sarcasm, succeeded in proving that the Old 'Un was inconsistent, immoral, forgetful, extravagant, and factious. But exactly a week later the Old 'Un got back his own, for he turned the Salisbury Government out neck and crop, and Churchill never introduced an Indian Budget.

I always thought that Lord Salisbury and Lord Randolph treated Hicks-Beach rather shabbily after the victory of the Unionists in the summer of '86.

Churchill made himself Chancellor of the Exchequer and Leader of the House, and Beach was more or less forced to become Chief Secretary to the Lord Lieutenant. It would have been better for the Unionist Party, and for the Statesmen concerned, if Hicks-Beach had remained Chancellor of the Exchequer and Leader of the House, for though his want of sympathy and geniality did not make him an ideal leader, we should have been spared the tragedy of Churchill's fall.

The crown of Hicks-Beach's Parliamentary career came in 1895, when Lord Salisbury made him Chancellor of the Exchequer, under Mr. Balfour's leadership of the Commons. Lord Salisbury had had quite enough of Goschen as Chancellor of the Exchequer. It is a striking illustration of the difference between the finance of Downing Street and Lombard Street that Goschen, bred in the City, was one of the worst Chancellors of the Exchequer, frittering away surplus after surplus; while two of the best Finance Ministers of the last century were Harcourt and Beach, both bred in the families of the landed aristocracy.

Although as a country gentleman Beach opposed Harcourt's death duties with perfect sincerity, he was far too shrewd to attempt their repeal; and, indeed, those duties contributed largely to his success as a Chancellor of the Exchequer. Harcourt and Beach had a real liking and respect for each other, partly due, no doubt, to class feeling, but more largely to recognition of a quality common to both—namely, clear and courageous commonsense.

Beach had to finance Chamberlain's South African War, which he did with adroitness, though his performance seems child's play at this hour. Nothing could shake Beach's adherence to Free Trade, though he imposed a registration duty of two shillings on corn towards the end of the war. But with his usual clearness of judgment, Beach saw that Chamberlain's influence was rapidly rising to predominance: he divined, or was told, that the Colonial Secretary's conversion to Protection was approaching; and he prudently decided to retire.

When Lord Salisbury resigned, Beach accepted a peerage, and as Viscount St. Aldwyn endeavoured for many years to compose, like Nestor, the quarrels of his friends, receiving the reward of an earldom. His last employment in the public service was unhappy, but the fault was not his. In his seventy-ninth year, fretted by disease, he was appointed by Mr. Lloyd George to preside over a Treasury Committee for the regulation of fresh issues of capital during the war. It was a task demanding great industry, patience, and knowledge of complicated city business. With the loyalty of an old servant of the Crown he responded to a call which should never have been made on him, and which, when domestic affliction was added, broke the cord of life.

Lord St. Aldwyn belonged to a school of statesmen which has passed away. He never bowed the knee to the idols of democracy; he was incapable of a mean or dishonourable deed; and he had his full share of the pride, the justifiable pride, which characterises the vigorous and successful race of English country gentlemen.

Henry Labouchere

B

HENRY LABOUCHERE

FEW men, who have occupied no official position, filled so large a space in the public eye as Mr. Labouchere. He was indeed a rare combination of opposites. Belonging by birth to the upper class, and inheriting a large share in a Lancashire bank, he was an irreclaimable Bohemian and an advanced Radical. There is always something attractive about a man who, having been educated at Eton and Cambridge, and drawing £10,000 a year from bank shares, turns his back upon "the perfumed chambers of the great," and chooses to live with actors, journalists, and republicans. He seems to have a leg in both worlds, and while he retails to mortals the scandal of Olympus he is thought to speak what he knows. If to this mode of life such a man add the fearless denunciation, by tongue and pen, of abuses in high and low places, the attraction becomes influence and popularity.

Sir Francis Burdett played this game very well at the beginning of the nineteenth century, and Mr. Labouchere played it even better at its close, for he did not, like Sir Francis Burdett, turn Tory in his old age. The Laboucheres have been great people in the high finance of Amsterdam and in society at The Hague for more than a century. Henry eschewed the family trade of banking (except as a shareholder), and began life in the diplomatic service, where he was a thorn in the side of the Foreign Office. For Henry Labouchere was a born rebel; he could no more help being an Ishmael than he could help his decidedly Dutch physiognomy. His mind was of that irreverent, inquiring order which takes nothing for granted, and frequently assumes that everything established is an imposture. The exposure of humbugs and swindlers in all walks became the passion of Mr. Labouchere's life, and he rendered great service to society at considerable personal expense. There was not a begging-letter writer, or a bucket-shop keeper, or an extortionate money lender, or a religious quack, or a fraudulent company promoter, or a purveyor of obscenity in any guise, who did not await the weekly issue of *Truth* with rage and trembling.

As an exposer of fraud Mr. Labouchere must have disbursed large sums, though I have no doubt the circulation of his paper recouped him. But innumerable libel actions are not defended for nothing, and there must have been a large detective staff; for information, as Lord Salisbury once said of our secret service fund, is entirely a question of money. Nor should it be forgotten in an enumeration of his service to the public, that we owe it to Mr. Labouchere that Constitution Hill is now a public thoroughfare. " The courage of the man " as I once heard a speaker in Hyde Park exclaim, " in fighting the Queen, and all the bigwigs to open Constitution Hill !"

When we turn from the assailant of abuses and the terror of evil-doers to the political journalist and member of Parliament, the record is blurred by extravagance and rabid partisanship. It is impossible that so clear-headed a man of the world as Mr. Labouchere can have believed all that he used to say and write of the Tory leaders. He once accused Lord Salisbury of helping a titled criminal to escape from a warrant, and of telling a lie to cover his connivance. He was, of course, instantly suspended by the Speaker, and it is more than probable that the ebullition was calculated. This was not the only time that Mr. Labouchere offended the taste of the House of Commons, for in 1881, when Mr. Gladstone pronounced a funeral eulogy on Lord Beaconsfield, Mr. Labouchere's attack on the policy and career of the dead statesman was drowned by murmurs from all sides.

With these two exceptions Mr. Labouchere managed very tactfully to assert the most violent opinions without making enemies of his brother members. There have been journalists in the House of Commons who earned their living by turning their colleagues into ridicule—a gross abuse of the freemasonry of Parliament. Mr. Labouchere was too well-bred, as well as too good-natured, to make this mistake. The leaders on both sides Mr. Labouchere considered fair game, but he never attacked private members, however prominent or obnoxious.

Like Abraham Lincoln, he had a weakness for repeating or inventing coarse stories, which were not always amusing, but made him a favourite of the smoking-room. This was the more exasperating as he was a really witty man.

Lord Taunton was his uncle, and some one, wishing to be agreeable, said, " Oh, Mr. Labouchere, I have just heard your father make an admirable speech in the House of Lords." " Really ?" said Labouchere ; " my father has been dead some years, and I always wondered where he had gone to." On the floor of the House of Commons " the Christian member for Northampton " made no effect whatever. His speeches were as a rule mere *rèchauffés* of his articles in *Truth*, delivered in a languid drawl with the aid of bits of paper which he dropped one by one into his hat after use.

He once told me that he spoke to the reporters, and regarded his fellow members as rows of lay figures. " Until you get into that frame of mind," he said, kindly enough, to a youngster not of his own side, " you will never succeed in politics." But it was with a stylo in his hand, and a cigarette-holder in his mouth that Mr. Labouchere became great. The editor of *Truth* never got credit for the real excellence of his prose style simply because no one expects to meet with first-rate English in a society weekly. Mr. Labouchere used to write a great deal in his paper, sometimes " notes " and sometimes leaders. Though unsigned, his " copy " was unmistakable.

In directness, in simplicity, in terseness of wit and humour, Mr. Labouchere's prose was Voltairean : it was better than Cobbett's, for that great master of journalism spoiled his effects by exaggeration and violent vituperation. Good writing is so rare in the English press that it is a thousand pities these articles should be lost.

Mr. Labouchere had another conspicuous foible : in the words of a French moralist, " *il faisait une fanfaronnade des vices, dont il n'etait pas capable.*" He took so low a view of his fellows that out of mere good-fellowship he was bound to make himself out as bad as he conceived them to be, or rather worse.

Once, after a rubber was over, his partner pointed out that his play, though successful, was extremely risky, as the adversary might have held such-and-such a card. " I agree," said Labouchere, " but then I took the precaution of looking over his hand."

When he was City editor of the *World* (his first essay in journalism) he tried operating on the Stock Exchange, and to help his speculation would write up the shares of which he was a bull, and write down the shares of which he was a bear. After he was caught at these manœuvres by the publication of some letters never intended for the light of day, Labouchere blandly asked, " What greater proof can I give of my belief in the shares I write up than buying them ? Or what stronger evidence can there be of my disbelief in a share than my selling it ?"

He soon gave up speculating, however, being much too clever not to realize that he could not play against the professional financier. In the Home Rule days, between 1886 and 1895, Mr. Labouchere was plunged in intrigue, and it was he who first saw through Pigott, and induced the forger to confess to Sir George Lewis and himself by means which his nephew, Mr. Thorold, has related to us in his interesting biography. The correspondence between Mr. Labouchere and Mr. Chamberlain on the Home Rule Bill of 1886 is not edifying. Both correspondents begin by treating the political situation as a problem of chess. But Mr. Chamberlain quickly drew off, and occupied high ground.

Labouchere makes no secret of the fact that he did not care a rap about Ireland and the Irish, but only wanted to get them out of the way. " For my part, I would coerce the Irish, grant them Home Rule, or do anything with them, in order to make the Radical programme possible. Ireland is but a pawn in the game. If they make fools of themselves, it would be easy to treat them as the North did the South, rule by the sword, and suppress all representation " (Labouchere to Chamberlain, March 31, 1886, Thorold's *Life of Labouchere*, pp. 289-90).

What is almost incredible, but is true, is that this clear-sighted cynic, this laughing philosopher, who wrote himself down an unprincipled trifler, was really disappointed because Mr. Gladstone did not ask him to join his Cabinet in 1892, and genuinely offended because he was not, in the alternative, sent as Ambassador to Washington ! The first refusal he put down to the Queen, and the second to Lord Rosebery, whom he pursued in *Truth* with unrelenting abuse. Such are the " follies of the wise "! Labouchere was what our neighbours used to call *trés fin de siécle* ; he was a very clever and amusing personality, whose withdrawal from politics and journalism left us all sadder men.

Mr. Bennett, the editor of *Truth*, has told the public, that his former editor-proprietor, was perfectly indifferent to what became of his copy after it had left his pen. When he retired to Florence, in the last years, he wrote much for his journal, but much of it was so irrelevant that it had to go into the wastepaper basket ; yet Labouchere never complained, or perhaps did not perceive it. Few, very few of the touchy tribe of journalists achieve so serene a philosophy.

… Charles Stewart Parnell

CHARLES STEWART PARNELL

Despite the Turkish proverb that " he who washes a blackamoor loses his soap," the fascination of cleansing the reputed villains of history seems perennial. Horace Walpole discovered that Richard the Third was a handsome and patriotic prince. H. B. Irving strove hard in a thick volume to make us believe that Judge Jeffreys was the victim of a ruthless monarch and a stone in the bladder.

Such attempts are comparatively safe when the rescued hero lived several centuries ago. Mr. St. John Ervine has used all the skill of the novelist and dramatist to persuade us that Parnell was not so black as he was painted, and that, beneath his cold brutality, there burned a steady, if tiny, flame of tenderness and purity. Would it not have been more prudent to wait until the death of the few Victorians who saw the man in the flesh before attempting to clothe his bones in a patchwork of apology made up from various books ?

I sat opposite Parnell in the House of Commons for six years, from 1885 to 1891. Parnell's head was the handsomest I ever saw, resembling somewhat Leonardo's imagination of Christ, with short yellow beard and brownish hair. His figure was tall, but clumsy and drooping, or perhaps it seemed so because of the ill-fitting clothes.

On rare occasions Parnell appeared in a black frock coat, not the smart production of Savile-row still worn by the elderly at functions, but in what used to be called a Sunday-go-to-meeting coat, shiny and shapeless. Generally he wore a brownish cutaway, with trousers of Irish homespun, baggy at the knees. All his pockets bulged with bulky things, probably a revolver, unopened letters and socks, for he was always changing his lodgings. His voice was that of the cultured upper class, and he used a low note, except when the hatred of his audience became uncontrollable, and you detected a fine tenor timbre. His vocabulary was meagre and commonplace, and his short speeches were frozen passion.

The general impression was one of high-bred refinement. If you had known nothing of the dirty things he did, you would have said, " behold a *pukka sahib*, who is surely entitled to trample on those who obey him !" Alas, there was very little refinement about the realities of Galway, Brighton, and Eltham. Nature plays sad tricks with our faces. Most Madonnas were painted from wantons. His habits were those of one who is wanted by the police. He lived under different names in different squalid streets.

It is seldom that the duality of the human character, the struggle between heredity and environment, is displayed in so fierce a light as in the case of Charles Stewart Parnell. You could almost see the wretch fighting against the Atè of a family malady. He was born in the bosom of " the Pale," a son of the proudest and most exclusive aristocracy in the world, with an unquenchable contempt for the conquered Irish Celt. His father lived like an Irish squire before the Lever tradition became extinct, in the open air and an open house.

As a young man " Charley " was fond of shooting, hunting, cricket, and dancing, especially the latter, for his amorousness declared itself early. Quarrelsome, argumentative, and domineering he always was with other boys, and ever rebellious against pastors and masters. But so little did his neighbours suspect him of disloyalty to his own class and creed that he was High Sheriff of Wicklow at the hour when he first talked of standing for Parliament; and everybody in the county assumed that he was coming forward as a Tory landlord.

What was the invisible and inexplicable agency which soured his nature in a night, and changed the squire into a raging Nationalist, the bitterest and most dangerous enemy England ever had to fight? He suffered no individual wrong, and he knew nothing of Irish history. But there was madness on both sides of the family.

His great-uncle, Sir Henry Parnell, was a distinguished speaker and writer on finance, a member of Parliament, and of Lord Grey's Government. In recognition of his services he was made an English peer, taking his title of Congleton from Cheshire, whence the Parnells migrated to Ireland in the seventeenth century. Almost immediately after his creation Lord Congleton committed suicide. Parnell's mother, Delia Stewart, was the granddaughter of an admiral who had fought against England in the Colonial rebellion, and she was as full of the venom of imaginary wrong as only Anglo-Americans of that type can be.

There can be no doubt that the daily dropping of her insane hatred of England sank into a young and unbalanced mind. Anna Parnell, one of the sisters, was an epileptic, and finally drowned herself. These two women goaded Parnell like gadflies, and he was himself afraid of going mad.

Parnell did not hate England as much as he despised the instruments of his senseless rage. Like most shy men, with a frigid manner, Parnell was full of family pride. He thought the Parnells the equals of the Cavendishes and the Churchills, while the smug airs of the British middle class infuriated him.

If either the Whigs or the Tories had received Parnell on his first appearance with courtesy, it has always been my belief that he would have come to terms. He was obviously pleased when Randolph Churchill opened some futile negotiations with him, and he even said: " I like Churchill." What stung him to the quick was to be classed by the House of Commons with the Harringtons and the Leamys. What else could he expect? We knew nothing of the Parnells of Wicklow. We only saw him at first as the coadjutor of a hunchback pork-butcher, who succeeded in destroying the rules of Parliamentary cricket. Later we were to know him as something sinister.

Parnell had a right to be angry at the heartless way in which the Liberals used him as a pawn in their game. Gladstone's settled policy for Ireland and Irishmen was caresses and coercion. He threw Parnell into Kilmainham Jail because he would not denounce outrages—Parnell said openly that he wouldn't do Gladstone's police work for him. While he was still in prison, Gladstone and Chamberlain began negotiations for his release, and the go-between was Mrs. O'Shea, who has told us in her book that the Grand Old Man knew all along the nature of her relations with Parnell.

When Mr. J. H. Morgan asked Lord Morley whether this was true, the answer was: " I dare say he did. Mr. G. was a man of the world." Now there is adultery and adultery. Lord Granville told Morley that he knew five of Queen Victoria's Prime Ministers who had committed adultery. But they wore their rue with a difference. Parnell not only seduced his friend O'Shea's wife, but he shared her possession with the husband, playing a game of Box and Cox at the Eltham villa, so that, until the divorce case, O'Shea believed that Parnell's three children were his own. Surely that is beyond the toleration of the man of the world, if not of the Liberal politician.

When Parnell entered the House of Commons after the Commission of Judges had pronounced the Pigott letters to be forgeries, the whole Liberal Party rose to their feet, waving their hats and cheering. Harcourt looked sour; Labouchere smiled impishly; they knew their Parnell, and felt they were making fools of themselves. The Grand Old Man opened his mouth and bayed like a bloodhound. Parnell's insolent indifference was the finishing touch to a contemptible scene.

A year later the Divorce Court revealed to the world the squalid and ludicrous details of the *crime passionel*, which had for years been known to every member of Parliament. Gladstone did not hesitate for an hour before throwing Parnell to the wolves. Look at him from whatever angle you will, Parnell was a bad man. It has been said that he rendered enormous service to the cause of Home Rule. It is not true. After his death in 1891, the Irish Nationalist Party was in a worse position than in 1879, when he drove its former leader Butt out of Parliament into the grave.

Viscount Grey

VISCOUNT GREY

The note in Sir Edward Grey's character which struck Prince Lichnowski, the German Ambassador, was simplicity, the frugality of his household, the plainness of his speech and manner. " On the few occasions when he entertained guests it was at a simple dinner or lunch, with maid-servants to wait. "

Lord Grey alludes in his *Twenty-five Years* to one of these dinners, to which he invited Hardinge and Haldane to meet Benckendorff, the Ambassador, and Isvolski, the Foreign Minister, and he didn't know whether these Russian grandees would take the homeliness of the entertainment as a compliment or a slight. " My manner of living had every comfort, but there was no state about it, no formality, no menservants, no party." Luckily the stroke succeeded, and Isvolski said to Benckendorff as they went away together, " I believe what you told me, these people are really friendly." Once when Grey lunched with Lichnowski, and heard his children talking German, he said, " I can't help thinking how clever these children are to talk German so well," and was pleased with his joke.

These are pleasant traits ; a very different side was shown to the House of Commons. When Campbell-Bannerman formed his Government in 1905 he offered the Foreign Office to Sir Edward Grey, then a

* *Twenty-Five Years*, 1892-1916, by Viscount Grey of Falloden. Two Vols. Hodder and Stoughton.

young man just over forty who had never been in a Cabinet. Grey went to the Prime Minister, who was over seventy, and told him that he must take a peerage and leave Asquith to lead the House of Commons, or otherwise he (Grey) would refuse to join the Government! Yielding to the solicitations of his friends, including the Prime Minister, the young man condescended to accept the Seals. Neither at the time, nor, writing twenty years afterwards, does Lord Grey betray the slightest consciousness that his conduct was unusual, not to say outrageous.

If he was arrogant to his elders and betters, Sir Edward Grey maintained towards the House of Commons a contemptuous reserve which froze his critics into silence. His short speech on August 3rd, when he told his countrymen in the unadorned language of an English gentleman that they must fight, placed him on a pinnacle from which he has never been dislodged.

Lord Grey laughs at long views in diplomacy, and ridicules the subtle and far-seeing policy which outsiders and the Press so often ascribe to statesmen. He contends that events make diplomacy, instead of diplomacy making events, as is commonly supposed.

After their experience of the touchiness and pinpricking of French Governments, Lord Salisbury and Mr. Joseph Chamberlain did seriously incline to an understanding, if not an alliance, between England and Germany. Lord Salisbury was willing to share with Germany the reversion of Portuguese possessions in Africa, and Mr. Chamberlain in his celebrated

VISCOUNT GREY

From Vanity Fair

Leicester speech sketched a triple alliance between America, England, and Germany, a grand entente between Teuton and Anglo-Saxon, which was to secure the peace of the world.

That, however, was the last thing which Germany desired. After repeated rebuffs, and the Kaiser's behaviour over South Africa, Lord Lansdowne turned in 1904 towards the friendship of France, beginning it with an arrangement for the distribution of the French and British fleets. Two years later, when Sir Edward Grey succeeded to Lord Lansdowne, those famous " conversations and understandings " between the military authorities of France and England were initiated. Neither country was pledged to the other, but their staffs consulted maps and exchanged views as to a possible combination of fighting forces.

When the war barometer pointed to " stormy," as at Algeciras in 1906, and over Agadir in 1911, the military and naval conversations naturally became more frequent and earnest, although their existence was never formally brought before either the country or the Cabinet until 1912. Lord Grey, looking backwards, makes an admission, an important one for him, that the military and naval conversations agreed on in 1906 should have been formally brought to the notice of the Cabinet before 1912.

Lord Grey confides to us, rather casually, as if it did not matter, that if England had not decided to fight independently of the Belgian question, he would have resigned; and that if Belgium had not been invaded England would not have gone into the war.

This shows Lord Grey's attitude to have differed from that of his colleagues in the Cabinet, and the majority of his countrymen. He, Lord Grey, would have declared war upon Germany, as soon as Germany declared war upon Russia, in order to save Europe from the domination of Germany, which he regarded as fatal to Western civilization. He does not allow that the message from Lord Lansdowne and Mr. Bonar Law, on August 2nd, promising Unionist support in the event of war, had any influence on the decision of the Cabinet, though he appreciates the spirit of the offer.

On the familiar question of whether an early intimation of British policy would have stopped the Germans from going to war, the British Foreign Secretary has a right to be heard with respect.

Lord Grey makes two very good points in reply to those who assert that if only the Government had told the Germans that they would stand by France, peace would have been preserved. If the understanding, and *a fortiori* an alliance, between England and France had been avowed at an early date, opinion both in the Cabinet and in the country would have been divided, and instead of meeting the enemy with a united front when war came, we should have had pacifists on one side and militarists on the other.

This is very true. We can well understand, from the shameful agitation against Lord Roberts, how certain school of politicians would have organised an opposition to all interference in European affairs.

The second point is based upon post-war German publications. The certainty of Britain coming in would not have prevented war, because the military party calculated on it as a possibility, and allowed for it in their plan. So much so, Lord Grey tells us, that the German Staff instructed the Navy not to interfere with the landing of our Expeditionary Force, which would be faithfully dealt with by the German troops.

The Kaiser and his Chancellor would possibly, or rather probably, have been affected by an assurance of British intervention, but they were not masters of the situation.

The deplorable slackness of British diplomacy at Constantinople which allowed Germany to replace us in the eyes of the Turk, even to the extent of a secret treaty between the Kaiser and the Sultan, is slurred over by Lord Grey, who goes out of his way to praise our Ambassador.

But with characteristic candour he admits that his Balkan diplomacy after war broke out was at fault. The refusal of Greece's offer to join the Entente for fear of pushing Turkey and Bulgaria into the arms of Germany was proved by the event to be a blunder. Lord Grey confesses that he was wrong about Bulgaria, and that the French scepticism, which knew Ferdinand for a fox, was the greater wisdom.

The trying to bribe Bulgaria, the attempt to form a new Balkan Confederacy, the persuading of Serbia not to arm against Bulgaria are all frankly set down with post-war wisdom on the debit side of the account.

The conclusion is that war was inevitable from the day when Germany began to build a big fleet. Security in the future depends not on pacts, but on persuading people not to pile up armaments. In civil and individual affairs security depends on the knowledge that if you break the law by injuring the life or property of another, the police will catch and the magistrates punish you.

Can you induce this state of mind amongst nations? That is, can you persuade them to substitute for the piling up of armaments confidence in and obedience to some international court of justice? Unless you can do this there can be no security for the future. And to do this you must establish a court with power to enforce its judgments.

The Earl of Oxford

THE EARL OF OXFORD AND ASQUITH
From Vanity Fair

THE EARL OF OXFORD

Herbert Henry Asquith was born in 1852, and belongs to that class of men, more common in the north than in the south of England, who come to grips with life at the very earliest opportunity. There is no preliminary lounging, no sowing of wild oats, no coquetry with the various forms of destiny. And these Yorkshire and Lancashire lads are right, for Fortune is " the easy mistress of the young," and prefers audacity to dalliance.

Asquith, a Fellow of Balliol, took his first in Greats in 1874, was called to the Bar in 1876, and married in 1877. He was elected to Parliament for East Fife in 1886.

It is a maxim in the profession that a junior, who enters Parliament without a practice big enough to justify his application for silk, is imperilling his future. As Asquith, a " stuff " of ten years standing, had little or no practice, and a wife and four children, it was a hazardous step. Nor did the new member look particularly happy at this time. His countenance was pale and ascetic ; he was dressed neatly but unfashionably ; his collars were of the wrong shape, and into peculiarly cut diagonal trouser-pockets he would thrust one hand when speaking, a stiff and awkward figure. He was content if the Speaker called him on

Wednesday, the private members' day of those times corresponding to Friday of to-day.

On one such occasion, I remember, he was answering the writer with the well-thumbed platitudes of Victorian Liberalism, when suddenly a loud, sweet voice, from the heights behind, cut across the monotonous humming with, " Mr. Speaker, this is a swindling speech." Members turned to a high back-bench to behold a tall figure on his legs in a brown suit and crimson tie (in those days an unusual costume), with pointed Vandyke beard, and white face surmounted by a shock of chestnut hair, and pierced by sparkling eyes. A murmur of " Cunninghame Graham " ran round the House, and Speaker Peel mildly observed that the interruption was not couched in parliamentary terms. But Leviathan was not so tamed.

In a louder voice Mr. Cunninghame Graham repeated, " I denounce this as a swindling speech," and as the Speaker was about to name him, he pointed a long artistic finger at the Chair, and cried in a voice that might have rent the Temple, " I appeal to the son of the man who gave the people free bread to give me free speech." Peel was visibly pleased, but was obliged to ask the offender to withdraw, which he did with grace and dignity.

I never could make out what Mr. Cunninghame Graham was driving at, for Mr. Asquith's speech did not strike me as more dishonest than that of most other Liberal politicians. Three years later, in 1890, he took silk, another bold step, against the advice of his friends at the Bar, as he has told us himself. A briefless Q.C. of fourteen years standing, surely he was taking great risks ! He was, but in another two years Mr. Gladstone, understanding that he was willing to quit his profession for politics, was writing to ask him to move a vote of no confidence in the defunct Salisbury Government, and a few days later he was Home Secretary, and not forty years of age.

Like most rapid successes in politics it was not so miraculous as it seemed. Sir Henry, afterwards Lord James, Attorney General in 1880, took care of promising young Liberals in the profession, and spotted Bob Reid, afterwards Lord Chancellor Loreburn, and Asquith, who devilled for him unofficially. Asquith wrote an opinion for him on some important political issue, and Henry James took care that the opinion and the name were brought under Mr. Gladstone's notice. The first push off in life is everything : the rest must be left to the man himself.

Asquith certainly did credit to the discernment of Henry James, for he was not only a courageous Home Secretary during the three years of Gladstone's last Administration, but his parliamentary speaking, logical, incisive, with a copious and correct vocabulary, was of the very highest order. Notwithstanding all this smooth ascent, it is doubtful what Asquith's future would have been during the ten years exile which the Liberal Party endured after the fall of Lord Rosebery's Government in 1895, had he not in the previous year taken a more important step than quitting the Bar. In 1891 Asquith's first wife died and in 1894 the thane of Fife took a second wife.

At the end of the last century knowledge of London society was still essential for influence in the House of Commons. Into those magic portals Margot Tennant, his young, beautiful, and witty wife, drew Asquith, who for the next decade was steeped to the lips in the political intrigues and intellectual pleasantry of a powerful set in the inner ring of the capital, then at the apex of its social glory. Harcourt, Rosebery, and Morley squabbled furiously, and a trio of understudies was formed by Asquith, Grey and Haldane. These three younger statesmen were followers of Rosebery and were very anxious not to be taken for Little Englanders. Asquith and Haldane had the wit to keep in with Campbell-Bannerman, whom the Whig, Sir Edward Grey, treated with disdain.

After ten years of Opposition it was a very different Asquith that emerged, rosy and regenerate, to take his place as Chancellor of the Exchequer in the Cabinet of 1905, an altogether mellowed and sapient statesman. During the first two years the new Government spent its magnificent majority in quarrelling with the House of Lords, who foolishly enough refused to recognise the fact of that majority. Then in 1908 Campbell-Bannerman died, Mr. Asquith became Prime Minister at the age of 56; and Mr. Lloyd George became Chancellor of the Exchequer.

I met Mr. Haldane at a dinner party just at this time, where he was surrounded by a little ring of

Tories, voicing their alarm at an extreme Radical being given the control of the national purse. I shall never forget Mr. Haldane's superb gesture of reassurance. " You needn't be afraid. I know my attorney, my Welsh attorney." How little he knew him was proved by the Budget of 1909, which, though most of its ridiculous taxes were afterwards repealed by a Government of which Mr. Lloyd George was the head, struck a death blow to the landed aristocracy. The dissolution of 1910 considerably reduced the Liberal majority, and then a discovery was made. The Irish Nationalists had not voted for the Budget, and were beginning to say that it was time Home Rule was taken up again.

Gladstone had a fixed idea, which he confided amongst others to George Russell, that the maintenance of the Liberal Party in office was the only barrier against revolution; and as the Liberal Party seldom commanded a majority of English voters, the alliance with the Irish Nationalists was necessary in the interest of English peace and security. The syllogism is flawless, granted the major premiss. Anyway, it was a mighty convenient doctrine for the Liberal Party, and was piously held by Campbell-Bannerman and Mr. Asquith.

On the death of King Edward, it was borne in upon the mind of the Prime Minister that with a new Sovereign and a reduced majority in a new House of Commons, something must be done about the Irish vote, and nothing could be done about Irish Home

Rule without doing something to the House of Lords. "The fall from power," wrote Burke about Chatham, "canonises and sanctifies a great character." That can only be true of a statesman who does not attempt his own defence, as was the fashion of the eighteenth century. But nowadays when Ministers hasten to publish in the newspapers their autobiographies, they enter the zone of criticism of their own accord. No apology therefore is required for using the freedom of history on Lord Oxford's *Fifty Years of Parliament*, followed by his valedictory address to Scotland last autumn.

All expectation of revelations, confessions, or originality is soon dispelled by the discovery that a large part of these volumes consists of excerpts from the biographies and memoirs of Morley, Buckle, Gardiner and Spender, stitched together by the measured and penetrative prose of Lord Oxford. The book does not profess to be "detached and impartial": thank God for that! But the author assures us that if he has not attempted to hold the scales even, he has "not consciously tampered with the balance." The difference between conscious and unconscious defies the judgment of the critic.

Starting from 1868, twenty years before Mr. Asquith's election to the House of Commons, the review of the duel between Gladstone and Disraeli is conventional, and such as any intelligent young Liberal might have written. There is the stale sneer at the Treaty of Berlin as a futile sham, which was reversed almost as soon as signed. It is true that in 1881, before the breath was out of Beaconsfield's body, the Gladstone Government set about the reversion of their predecessor's Eastern policy. But even in its mutilated form the Treaty of Berlin kept the peace of Europe for thirty-six years.

Nor do I think that at this hour Lords Oxford and Grey can look back upon their Eastern policy with complacence.

The Eastern policy of Palmerston and Beaconsfield was to back Turkey against Russia and the Balkan States, because British supremacy at Constantinople was necessary to England as an Eastern Power. The policy of Gladstone and the Liberal Party was to back Russia and the Balkan States against Turkey because of the perfectly irrelevant fact that Russia and the Balkan States belonged to the Byzantine branch of the Roman Church. To Gladstone Russia was " the Divine figure from the North," and this irrational religious sentiment imposed on so cool a statesman as Lord Salisbury, who joined the crusade against the Turk, and declared that " we had put our money on the wrong horse."

We all know now that Salisbury and Grey put us on a whole stable of wrong 'uns, and that Liberal foreign policy led straight to Armageddon. Had the traditional Eastern policy of Palmerston and Beaconsfield been adhered to, Turkey and Bulgaria would not have been German allies in 1914.

Mr. Asquith was one of Parnell's counsel before the

Special Commission, and chatting one day intimately, Parnell said : " It is a great mistake to suppose that Ireland cannot be governed by coercion." Mr. Asquith answered—a little shocked, we may imagine—that it was their common creed that coercion had been proved impossible. " Perhaps it has," replied Parnell. " but that is not because the task is impossible in itself ; it is because, under your English party system, neither party can be trusted to make the policy continuous, whatever Government may be in power." What a flashlight upon the humbug of conciliation and coercion ! It is precisely Lord Salisbury's " twenty years of resolute government," which the Unionists did apply to Ireland between 1885 and 1905, with a brief interlude. In 1905 the Unionist Government handed over Ireland to the Liberals in a state of rising prosperity and contentment. In three or four years the Liberal Government thrust its fingers into the healing wound, and ripped it open for the basest purposes of party.

In a vivid stroke Lord Oxford gives us a glimpse of Gladstone's last Cabinet. " Lord Kimberley, who was genuinely moved, had uttered a few broken sentences of affection and reverence, when Harcourt produced from his box and proceeded to read a well-thumbed MS of highly elaborate eulogy. Of those who were present there are now few survivors ; but which of them can forget the expression of Mr. Gladstone's face as he looked on with hooded eyes and tightened lips at this maladroit performance ?" That Gladstone should afterwards have referred to " the blubbering Cabinet " which " put him out " shows how insensible to all sentiment are very old people.

Mr. Asquith and his colleagues would have been more than human if they had not gleefully watched, with steady beating of the Free Trade drum, the dying struggles of the Unionist Party under the dual control of Messrs. Balfour and Chamberlain. Even down the long vista of years the vision of the " Madonna lily " worn in the buttonhole of the tearing, raging campaigner is humiliating.

During the years between 1906 and 1913 Mr. Asquith was solely, or mainly, responsible for the following disservices to the State : The Trades Disputes Act, 1906 ; The Payment of Members ; The Naval Prize Bill of 1910 ; The Parliament Act, 1911 ; The Trade Union Funds (political levy) Act, 1913. I doubt if any other Prime Minister (not excluding Lord Liverpool), has so heavy a debit balance, for I challenge anyone to deny that each and all of the abovementioned measures were of signal disservice to the State. The Trades Disputes Act, *to which in two volumes Lord Oxford allots exactly ten words*, together with the Political Levy Act of 1913, constitutes that charter of licence and anarchy which places the funds of the trade unions beyond liability for the acts of their members, legalizes picketing, and allows the officials to divert subscriptions for benefit to political purposes.

All our industrial troubles of the last twenty years,

including the general strike and the coal strike, are due to the Acts of 1906 and 1913. The Naval Prize Bill, *of which Lord Oxford makes no mention whatever*, incorporated The Declaration of London, 1909, the result of the Hague Conference, and was carried through the House of Commons in 1910. Had it passed the Lords, it would have literally lost us the war, for it made a blockade impossible, and deprived Britain of every rag of naval power in war left us by the Declaration of Paris, 1856. Happily, it was rejected by the House of Lords, whose patriotic courage was rewarded in the following year by the Parliament Act, which was carried by the threat, made with the King's sanction, of a catastrophic creation of peers.

Lord Oxford in his valedictory address to the electors of Scotland harped on the Parliament Act as the crowning achievement of his life. This is provocative, as most people regard it, especially by the light of recent events, as the least justifiable measure of his Premiership. " It was the Government of which I was at the head which, by means and by means only of the Parliament Act, was able to put Home Rule, thrice approved by the electorate of the country, upon the Statute Book." When was Home Rule thrice approved by the electorate after its repudiation in 1895 ? Certainly not in the General Election of 1905, which was won by " Rome on the rates," Free Trade, and " the terminological inexactitude " about Chinese labour, Home Rule being sedulously kept in the background.

The election of 1909-1910 was fought on the single issue of Mr. Lloyd George's Budget; and the second election of the same year 1910-11 was based on a vague and undefined demand for the reform of the House of Lords. Lord Oxford indeed admits, most incautiously, that his sole object in mutilating the ancient constitutional power of the second Chamber was to carry a Home Rule Bill, which was never made operative.

What was his mandate for this revolutionary step? It is not realized, or remembered, that Liberals and Conservatives were exactly divided in the constituencies on the question of House of Lords Reform, as it was put to the electors. The figures of the 1910 election were: Liberals 272; Conservatives 272; Irish Nationalists 84; Labour members 42. The Irish Nationalists, to whom the House of Lords was sold, must be left out of the account. So that Mr. Asquith's warrant for violating the constitution was the vote of 42 Labour Socialists.

In England there was a majority of 23 against dealing with the House of Lords and Home Rule. Clause 1 of the Parliament Act runs as follows: " If a money Bill having been passed by the House of Commons and sent up to the House of Lords at least one month before the end of the Session, is not passed by the House of Lords without amendment within one month after it is so sent up to that House, the Bill shall, unless the House of Commons direct to the contrary, be presented to His Majesty and become an Act of Parliament upon the Royal Assent being signified notwithstanding that the House of Lords have not consented to the Bill." A grosser affront, couched in terms of coarser contempt, has never been put upon one branch of the legislature by the other. Under these conditions the mere sending up of a money Bill to the Lords is an impertinence. It is also an injury to the nation, for there is no body that is more capable of criticising a money Bill, and whose amendments would be more valuable, than the House of Lords. With a few exceptions, such as the chairmen of Banks, all our financial magnates have been made peers, I sometimes think, to escape their criticism in the Lower House. In the republic of Florence, to ennoble a political opponent and so remove him from the arena, was a recognized stroke. If not the power of rejection, certainly the power of amending money Bills should be restored to the House of Lords. Their discussion would be invaluable, and the House of Commons would be shy of rejecting the amendments of men of authority in finance. The power of deciding what are Money Bills should be taken away from the Speaker, more clearly defined, and entrusted to a Committee of the two Houses, or perhaps to a judicial referee.

Everybody knows, and admits in private, that of the two Chambers the House of Lords is in every way superior, better for discussion and better for legislation. But just because it is not elected in a miscellaneous tumult of indifferent and ill-informed electors, the best Second Chamber in the world is bound and muzzled. Strangers who take the trouble to follow our politics must be amazed at British perversity, or the cowardice of our politicians.

Having deprived the House of Lords of its constitutional right to reject a Bill for the disruption of the Union, Mr. Asquith and his colleagues flung themselves heart and soul into the congenial work of bargaining with Mr. John Redmond and his party over the clauses of a Home Rule Bill, which, under the three years' veto, was to be placed on the Statute Book in 1914.

Three members of the Cabinet, the Prime Minister, Lord Chancellor Haldane, and Sir Edward Grey, the Foreign Secretary, must have felt very uncomfortable. Haldane had been to Berlin in 1912, and there had been deployed for his benefit (he was then Secretary for War) the largest, best equipped, and best disciplined army in the world. The Kaiser patronized him; Admiral Von Tirpitz was as rude to him as only a Prussian official can be; and he had declined the insulting proposition that England should bind herself to remain neutral in the event of a war with France.

After 1912 the trio could have been under no illusion. They must have realized, if nobody else did, that " murder with its silent bloody feet " was ever creeping nearer. Haldane sent a circular memorandum to the members of the Cabinet giving an account of his mission to Berlin, which they apparently neglected to read, so much more exciting was Ulster's resistance to the Home Rule Bill. Belfast was more interesting than Berlin. Mr. Churchill, First Lord of the Admiralty, declared that " the time had come to put these grave matters to the touch," and cabled to the ships, but recalled his cable. General Seely, Secretary for War, bethought him of the King's troops at the Curragh, but learnt that the officers would not fight Ulster.

There were famous debates in Parliament, and recourse was finally had to Buckingham Palace conferences. When the army of Mahomet II was advancing upon Constantinople, the Latins and Greeks were preoccupied with a dispute over the Union of the Churches of Rome and Byzantium; and, in their furious discussions of the rival merits of Pope and Patriarch, neglected to make any preparations for a siege. In January 1914 the Chancellor of the Exchequer, Mr. Lloyd George, announced that our relations with Germany were better than they had been for a long time, and that the time was propitious for a reduction of expenditure on armaments. The Chancellor of the Exchequer was not one of the triumvirate, and like Lord Morley and Lord Loreburn, who after the war wailed angrily that " they had never been told," presumably had not read the Haldane Memorandum.

But the uneasiness of the triumvirate must have been growing intense. They knew that the country was quite unprepared; and they were afraid to take the people into their confidence, for England had not only no army, but no policy. They strove to console themselves in their secret conclaves by Lord Haldane's assurance that preparation for war would precipitate its declaration. Yet there were signs in addition to the insolence of Berlin, which ought to have convinced any man at the centre of things.

In May the Rothschilds brought out a Hungarian Gold Loan. All through June and July there was heavy selling of securities on the London Stock Exchange by the Deutsche Bank, and the Dresdner Bank, and the brokers who deal for German clients. This emptying of portfolios on to the ignorant British investor must have carried a terrible message to the triumvirate, who had not even then made up their minds. On Friday, 31st July, three days before England's ultimatum to Germany, and after Austria's invasion of Serbia, and Germany's declaration of war on Russia and France, the President of the French Republic wrote a letter to the King of England, imploring him to say whether France could count upon him to stand by her side.

This was the answer His Ministers caused the King of England to send two days before the ultimatum: "I. August 1914. Buckingham Palace. Dear and Great Friend,—As to the attitude of my country, events are changing so rapidly that it is difficult to forecast future developments; but you may be assured that my Government will continue to discuss freely and frankly any point which might arise of interest to our two nations with M. Cambon—GEORGE R. and I."

Such was the picture of the British nation which Mr. Asquith's Government bade the King-Emperor hang out to the world! For pompous and cold futility can it be beaten? Then came Sunday. I take the following description from Mr. J. H. Morgan's book on Lord Morley, p.44. " On August 2nd, a Sunday, I think," (a touch of Morley, that) " we went to lunch at Beauchamp's—Lloyd George, Simon and myself. Simon said to me before we went up stairs, ' I think I've got L.G. He is with us.' The next day—half an hour before the Cabinet met—I said to L.G. ' I'm going.' He replied, ' Don't be in a hurry.' Half an hour later he said, ' I stay. It's Belgium.' Simon resigned with tears streaming down his face at having to leave Asquith. The same evening Burns came to me and said ' Simon's going to stay—he's withdrawn his resignation'." That same Sunday there arrived, while the Cabinet was sitting, a letter signed by Lansdowne and A. Bonar Law, pledging the support of the Unionist Party in the event of the Government going to war.

Lord Grey, in his memoirs denies that this letter had any effect upon the decision of the Cabinet, and Lord Oxford in his *Fifty Years* does not mention it. The next day, Monday, all trace of indecision disappeared, and the resignations of Lord Morley and Mr. Burns were announced. Mr. Asquith and Sir Edward Grey made speeches worthy of the occasion and of English statesmen. On Tuesday, the 4th of August, midnight, England was at war.

In 1916 Mr. Asquith allowed himself to be intrigued out of Downing Street by his lieutenant, Mr. Lloyd George, aided and abetted by his (Asquith's) personal friends.

Who that beheld the first Coalition, which Mr. Asquith, in an access of nerves, formed in 1915, could have suspected its solidity, or questioned its beauty? It was composed of all the cleverest men from the two parties, and the man in the street was comforted by the thought that here at least was a Government free from personal rivalries, that must endure till the hour of victory.

Eighteen months slipped away, and I was so much impressed by the outward show that I wrote an article in *The Fortnightly Review* of October, 1916, comparing Mr. Asquith to Burleigh, and describing him as "the indispensable Premier." Within three weeks Mr. Asquith was leaving the Reform Club with tears in his eyes and rage in his heart, a fallen Minister, followed by Sir Edward Grey, Sir Herbert Samuel and many other Liberal Statesmen.

> " Keen were his pangs, but keener still to feel,
> He nursed the pinion which impelled the steel."

The only man who told me what was going to happen a week before the event was Lord Alexander Thynne, killed shortly afterwards in Flanders. The secret was well kept, and the plans of the plotters complete to the last button. Mr. Bonar Law, the leader of the largest English party, gave way to Mr.

Lloyd George, all "according to plan." The most surprising part of the business was that the Unionist leaders had proffered support to Mr. Asquith, and spoken of Mr. Lloyd George in terms of depreciation, or something worse. Yet when the pinch came, they one and all joined the Government of Mr. Lloyd George.

The spectators saw nothing of all this underplay. They were told by their papers that Mr. Asquith was slow, and Mr. Lloyd George was quick, and that what Mr. Joseph Chamberlain called "push and promptitude" would shortly end the war. But did the spectators know, or were they told, that at the very hour when Mr. Lloyd George leaped into Mr. Asquith's seat a definite offer of peace had arrived from the Emperor of Austria? The Prince Sixte de Bourbon, the brother of the Empress, arrived with an autograph letter from Charles offering to withdraw from the war if the Allies would guarantee his empire against Germany.

If Austria had pulled out of the war, Bulgaria and Turkey must have followed, and Germany's flank or rear being uncovered, peace must have ensued in the beginning of 1917. Anyone can imagine how an Austrian Ambassador of peace would be received in Italy, which had been bribed to come into the war by promises of Austrian, Greek, and Turkish territory. Or in Paris, where *jusqu' àboutisme* raged like a madness.

Mr. Lloyd George ordered the Emperor's brother-in-law to be quite genially received in the Downing Street ante-room. He sent out for the letter to read by himself, and to amuse the Prince he instructed one of his secretaries to offer him a cigar, which the Bourbon described, in his printed story, as of indifferent quality. That afternoon or the next day our Prime Minister told the Emperor's envoy that whatever his own view of the offer, the Allies wouldn't hear of it, and that " Sonnino was very violent."

As Mr. Lloyd George had just been made Premier on the knock-out-blow ticket, what chance had the unfortunate Charles of being listened to? The Austrian Emperor may have been mistaken, and his proposals may have been impracticable. But at least the peoples of Italy, France and Britain might have been allowed to decide upon the facts. Of all these things, of this most sinister piece of underplay, the spectators were not allowed to catch a glimpse. It was not until four years after the peace that the Prince Sixte's narrative was published.

To this day I have never understood why Mr. Asquith did not fight Mr. Lloyd George. His first blunder was in May, 1915, when everybody lost his head over the shortage of ammunition, which was common to all the belligerents; and as far as England was concerned, the blame lay, not on the Government, not on the Ordnance Department, or Lord French or Lord Kitchener, but on the armament firms and the trade unions. And not entirely on them. At the time when Mr. Asquith was apologising and Lord French was complaining of the want of high explosive shells, it was a fact that they could not be fired without bursting our field-guns, a defect which was shortly afterwards remedied at Woolwich Arsenal.

The formation of the first Coalition was a mistake, not only because it deprived the Government of the intelligent criticism of a patriotic Opposition, but because it led to the second Coalition of 1916, and to the third Coalition of 1918, the two rashest and most corrupt governments this country has ever seen. In December, 1916, under Mr. Asquith's newly passed Parliament Act, the legal life of Parliament had expired. Why did Mr. Asquith not appeal to the country ?

One of our Dominions, Canada or Australia, I forget which, had a General Election during the war, and ballot papers were delivered in the trenches. Mr. Asquith would then have got a majority, and could have used Mr. Lloyd George as Munition Minister, a job for which he was splendidly fitted. After reading Sir William Robertson's *Soldiers and Statesmen*, I have formed the opinion that Mr. Asquith was an infinitely better war Premier than Mr. Lloyd George.

Sir William Robertson's thesis is simple. Admitting that strategy cannot be dissociated from politics, the Field Marshal contends that the Cabinet must trust its technical advisers in tactics, or else change them. Mr. Asquith was accused of sluggishness, and of not calling a meeting of the debating club known as the War Council for six weeks. Mr. Asquith trusted his technical advisers, and was probably not desirous of hearing them talked down by Mr. Churchill. Was he not right? Mr. Lloyd George did not trust his technical advisers, and was afraid to change them. The most frightful risks were run in 1917 and in the early months of 1918, owing to shortage of men. If Mr. Asquith had dissolved in 1916, peace, I believe, would have come earlier, even if Italy had been obliged to go without some of her spoils, and Mr. Asquith and the Liberal Party would then have been the winners of the war.

But as Pascal drily observes, if Cleopatra's nose had been shorter, the history of the world would have been different.

Lord Oxford will be remembered in history as the author of the Parliament Act, which emasculated the best Second Chamber in the world. In the last years of Queen Anne's reign the Lord Treasurer was created Earl of Oxford. He ended badly, in the Tower of London, where one of the articles of impeachment exhibited against him was the creation of twelve peers to carry the Treaty of Utrecht. Almost exactly two centuries later the Prime Minister threatened to create 500 peers to carry the Parliament Bill. In both cases the Sovereign was used by a party chief to pass a partisan measure: and in both cases retribution ensued. Harley died a released prisoner. Mr. Asquith lost his party and his power, but the milder manners of the twentieth century have consoled him with an earldom and the Garter.

Politics apart, I hope that Lord Oxford may enjoy many years of the peace that is built on a guiltless conscience; but to that end he must so manage his memory that between Mr. Asquith and Lord Oxford—

"An everlasting Lethé flows,
Which whoso drinks forgets himself, his friends,
His former cause."

The Statesman's End

THE STATESMAN'S END

I HAVE been counting the number of Prime Ministers and statesmen of the front rank who, in the nineteenth century, ended their careers unhappily.

The second Pitt died in January 1806, at the age of forty-six. He had been conducting a war first against the Jacobins, and then against Buonaparte, for eleven years unsuccessfully. Twice his Continental coalitions, built up with so much diplomacy and money, had been broken up, and for months before his death he had gone about with the Austerlitz look in his face. He was an exceptionally proud man, and he inherited from Chatham a gouty diathesis with its attendant irritability. In the language of the times, he died of a broken heart. We should say he died of worry and failure, aggravated by alcoholism. Six years later, Spencer Perceval, Prime Minister by the grace of Eldon, was shot dead in the lobby of the House of Commons by a madman, who mistook him for Lord Granville Leveson, our Ambassador at St. Petersburg, against whom he thought he had a grievance. In the following eight years there were three terrible suicides.

Whitbread cannot perhaps be called a statesman; but he was leader of the Whig Opposition in the House of Commons when he cut his throat, worried by Drury Lane and political troubles. Samuel Romilly really was a great man, lawyer, philanthropist, and statesman; and he cut his throat, presumably in grief for his wife's death. The most gruesome end was Lord Londonderry's, who was the effective ruler of Liverpool's Cabinet, and one of the greatest Foreign Secretaries this country has ever had. He had been blackmailed for years in connection with an amorous misadventure, and as he was shaving one morning at his villa near Chislehurst he thought he saw his torturers walking up the avenue—they turned out to be ordinary respectable men. " Carotid-artery-cutting Castlereagh " was one of Byron's worst brutalities. Lord Liverpool had a paralytic stroke, and died a " driveller and a show." Canning, having at last attained the Premiership, was " chased and hunted to death " by the Die-hard Tories, led by Peel and Wellington, and by intriguing Whigs who would not support him on Catholic Emancipation, which they carried two years after his death.

Even as Peel and Wellington did unto Canning, so twenty years later (1846) was it done unto Peel by Bentinck and Disraeli. On the very night that Peel carried his Corn Bill in the House of Lords, he was turned out by a junction of Tory Protectionists with the regular Opposition in the House of Commons on an Irish Coercion Bill. Peel lived for five years in unhappy isolation, and perhaps remorse, and in 1851 was killed by falling off his horse on Constitution Hill. Three years previously Melbourne had slipped into wistful senility, and died " deserted by those his former bounty fed." Fourteen years later Abraham

The Statesman's End

Lincoln was murdered in a theatre by a fanatic's pistol.

There can be no doubt that Beaconsfield felt his defeat by Gladstone in 1880 very bitterly. He had been so much the idol of Europe since the Berlin Congress that he was deeply wounded by the failure of his own countrymen to appreciate his services. Although Disraeli had realised all the dreams of his boyhood, and although his health had been failing for some six or seven years, I shall always think that the General Election of 1880, which he did not survive more than a year, left him a lonely and disappointed old man, despite of the dinner parties which he attended till within a few weeks of his death. When he was asked whether he would care to see Bismarck, who was reported to be coming to London in '81, he said, " He would not care to see me now."

But was not the end of his great rival even more pathetic ? Foiled for the second and, as he knew, for the last time in his heroic endeavour to carry Home Rule, deaf, and with a most painful nasal trouble, Gladstone, as he said to himself, was pushed out of his own Cabinet, and lingered for four years to watch his own Party being shivered to atoms.

The death of Parnell in 1891 recalls Mr. Laurence Housman's *Dethronements*, for Parnell is one of the three dethroned kings, Randolph Churchill being, however, alluded to as a fourth. Mr. Housman's moral is that the greatest statesmen are always undervalued by their contemporaries, and pulled down by inferior but conventional politicians. Of Chatham and Beaconsfield this is true: their fame began, and is still growing after their death. But Mr. Housman is wrong in classing Parnell and Randolph Churchill as kings dethroned by misunderstanding contemporaries. Both were kings in the command of devoted followers and in the possession of daimonic energy. But both destroyed themselves by their passions and the violence of their personal hatreds.

Parnell looked and spoke like a king. But besides robbing one of his few friends of his wife, he was a vulgar polygamist, as Scotland Yard well knew. His love of Ireland was hatred of Englishmen, who exasperated him by their preference for decency, which he called hypocrisy. That is why Mr. Housman's last scene between Parnell and his wife is such terrible bathos: "nothing is here for tears." Lord Randolph Churchill's death at the age of 46 is far sadder, because he lagged on the stage of public life at least three years after the decay of his faculties must have been plain even to himself. But his son, who saved his own career by escaping from Arthur Balfour before it was too late, has written that tragedy. When Lord Iddesleigh (Sir Stafford Northcote) was finally made to understand in 1887 that he was no longer to be allotted his position of power in the Tory Party, he died on the sofa in the Foreign Office under Lord Salisbury's eyes, who wrote to a friend that he had never looked on a dead body before.

In Mr. Chamberlain's sick room at Highbury Mr.

Housman has succeeded in touching the pathetic chord more effectively, though even here bathos and pathos come perilously near to one another. For it appears that Joseph Chamberlain's last and most embittering obsession was that he, the business man, had been beaten at his own game, i.e. political deals and intrigues, by that charming dilettante, Arthur J. Balfour! The satire upon Lord Balfour is all the more deadly because it is so delicate as almost to persuade the reader that it is not meant. But there were others besides Joe Chamberlain who found themselves " left "—Wyndham and Cust, for instance—by the owner of that graceful manner and all-atoning smile. Like Tithonus, Chamberlain could not die, but lived eight years after his retirement in 1906, a helpless invalid. In spite of his partial aphasia, I am told he continued to curse the stupidity of the Tories.

It is difficult for Englishmen, the majority of whom do not understand the intricacies of the American Constitution, to put themselves into the skin of the unhappy Mr. Woodrow Wilson. The imaginary dialogue between the paralysed ex-President and Mr. Tumulty, his secretary throws some light on the situation. President Wilson, having proclaimed his Fourteen Points, including " freedom of the seas, no indemnities, no annexation," sailed for Europe in the firm conviction that they would be joyfully accepted by all the world. He knew nothing of any secret treaties, and he believed Mr. Lloyd George when he had promised " open diplomacy." As soon as he arrived in Paris and was taken into " the kitchen," the doors were locked, and he was shown the secret treaty of London, 1915, which gave so much to England, to France, to Italy, to Japan, to Serbia and to Greece. What was he to do ? Was he to swallow the partitions and indemnities, and concentrate on the League of Nations ? Or was he to wash his hands of the whole business and return to America ? What he ought to have done was to go home and take counsel with his Senate. What he did was to waste six months in drafting and signing a Peace Treaty and a Covenant, both of which were repudiated by the Senate and the American electors.

Not the least of the poignant tragedies of politics was that of Mr. Bonar Law in 1923. Since the death of W. H. Smith in 1891 I cannot recall any event which has been so personally grievous to politicians of all parties, both in Parliament and out of doors. Both men were respected and loved, not only by those who knew them, but by millions who had only read about them in the newspapers, for their sweetness of temper and honesty of conduct. Mr. Bonar Law and Mr. Baldwin broke up Mr. Lloyd George's Coalition Government in 1922. Mr. Bonar Law had received a serious medical warning as early as 1921 ; but the lure of politics, the intense desire to serve his country in the highest position, induced him to risk his life in an endeavour whose failure many foresaw.

In the beginning of 1923, he had been given by the country a majority which made him Prime Minister.

Within four months he resigned, and within a year he was dead. Mr. Bonar Law was hardly a great statesman. He had become leader of the Tory party in 1911, owing to Mr. Balfour's sudden and unexpected retirement. It was therefore by something of an accident that Mr. Bonar Law found himself at the head of the Unionists, and it is impossible to say how he would have discharged that function, had his health lasted. He was not an orator, either in Parliament, or on the platform; but he was a man round whose shrewdness, courage and honesty the confidence of the public was rapidly gathering.

There lingers another illustrious victim. Thirty-two years ago Lord Rosebery was Prime Minister for a year. He had won the Derby, and he was acknowledged to be the most finished orator of his time. In an evil hour it entered his head to speak the truth, and not to stick to it. He said that " England was the predominant partner." Had he stuck to it, he would have headed an Imperialist Party which might have endured to this day. Within twenty-four hours he was bullied by John Morley and the newspapers into recalling his words. From that moment the attributes of power began to fall from him. Lloyd George dubbed him " a soft-nosed torpedo "; and to-day he is the dignified wreck that is wheeled about the Durdans.

Soc
DA
550
B3